The authors of this heartfelt book have inspired me as a nurse practitioner/medical provider to work with eating disorder patients. They are professional, loving, and supportive human beings who are passionate about helping those who suffer with disordered eating. For years, Barbi has lectured on this serious and often frustrating illness throughout the United States, sharing her own story and knowledge, giving hope to professionals, patients, and families. Carrie has educated and supported individuals, families, students, and communities through treatment and prevention. Both authors share from their hearts and personal experiences, encouraging individuals looking for answers related to eating and body image questions.

Susan D. McEwen, MSN, Family Nurse Practitioner

Barbi Webber and Carrie Thiel have created a book that connects with readers by sharing their own life experiences and many tools to guide, educate, and support mindful living and self-reflection for those healing from disordered eating. The authentic messages and coping strategies they share are not invented; they were created by surviving self-destruction and ultimately finding the strength to return to life on a healthier path. My high school students respond to the endearing wisdom and insight contained in this book in positive and meaningful ways.

Kimberly Schneider, MA, Secondary Educator

Barbi and Carrie were crucial elements in our daughter's eating disorder recovery. Barbi was an amazing mentor, offering practical advice and specific strategies that helped with our daughter's day-to-day healing, but her wisdom as a survivor was the piece of the puzzle that made the biggest difference to our daughter. Barbi knows how horrible it feels to have an eating disorder, what a dark place it is. My daughter listened to Barbi's survival story and found hope in it. Carrie is an amazing counselor. She sees right through the patterns and excuses that people with eating disorders use and helps them get to work on healing. I cannot recommend this book highly enough.

Jim and Kristi Jore, Parents

Barbi and Carrie write as they live: thoughtfully, courageously, and from their hearts. Their insights illuminate the complexities of eating disorders—exploring personal, social, spiritual, and relational dimensions of these diseases that are so difficult for many to comprehend and therefore treat. By dismantling attitudes of secrecy, shame, and fear that often surround the discussion of disordered eating, the authors inspire a perspective of curiosity, hope, and possibility for positive transformation. Barbi and Carrie write personally and with love, while also providing scientific and research-based information. This book is a resource for anyone who is seeking a new and authentic voice in the conversation about eating disorders. It expands the discussion beyond a focus on individuals and a narrow perspective of eating patterns, inviting us to consider new opportunities to grow and become more conscious and whole in relationship to our bodies, food, and life.

Maryl Baldridge, MA, Licensed Massage Therapist, Yoga Instructor, and Co-owner of Georgetown Yoga

SURVIVING
DISORDERED EATING
One Bite at a Time

Barbi Webber
Carrie Thiel

ISBN: 978-1-60679-340-4
Library of Congress Control Number: 2015940805
Cover design: Cheery Sugabo
Book layout: Cheery Sugabo
Front cover photo: oliver wolfson/iStock/Thinkstock

Healthy Learning
P.O. Box 1828
Monterey, CA 93942
www.healthylearning.com

Dedication

We dedicate this book to:

My angel sister, DeeDee.

—Barbi

*My children, Claire and Kyle, and my grandchildren, Jude, Kila, and Kendall.
You are the hearts of my heart.*

—Carrie

Acknowledgments

Thank you, dearest Annie Crandall Campbell, for saving my life. This healing book would not exist without you. You were the person who stayed beside me, pounding on the door, asking me to stop throwing up in that bathroom. You encouraged me instead to play soccer, take a hike, shed some tears, dance. I cherish every heartbeat that we share. Your photos inspire us to become mindful of life's treasures above, below, and all around.

Thank you, my dear sister Sally. You are a true soul mate to me, blessing life with the joy and comfort of sisterhood that never needs explaining. We are kindred spirits linked by our angel sister, Dale, in mutual admiration, love, support, creativity, thoughtfulness, and wisdom earned by survival, faith-filled trust, and never-ending inspiration. I love you so!

Orrin, Blake, and Brie: Thank you for encouraging me to stand up and talk out loud about my eating disorder journey and to never sit down. Your unconditional love and support have been my inspiration to make a difference in another person's healing. I am forever grateful.

Oh Sam, thank you from the bottom of my heart for sitting together as we unlocked the expressions of eating disorder challenge and recovery captured in my journals over these past eight years of beloved Body Balance mentoring. Your intuition and experience have brought forth meaningful expressions that we captured with an all-knowing twinkle of the eye between us. It has meant the world to me to feel so comfortable beside you. I could not have done even a small portion of this piece without you, dear Sam.

Carrie, your written expressions have brought forth a healing light as a guide to the rebalancing journey out of disordered eating and its darkness. Thank you for blessing these pages with your gifts and talents as a compassionate writer. You especially helped my survival journey to become a passage that others could find, understand, and use to enhance their healing. My heart pounds with gratitude.

—Barbi Webber

First and foremost, thank you, Barbi, for inviting me to join you in sharing our voices in support of those working to overcome disordered eating. It has been extremely gratifying to collaborate with you on a project that, hopefully, will offer support and healing opportunities to many people.

It isn't easy being married to a writer. We can be moody, brooding, preoccupied, and silent at times. I so appreciate your quiet, constant, steady support, Mike. You are my rock.

Claire and Kyle: you have taught me every important truth I've ever learned. Thank you for the grace and generosity you bestow upon me daily. Claire, thank you for sharing your story and poems. They speak truth, like you do.

Mom and Dad: for the gift of life and love—thank you.

To my Wolf Sisters (my writing group), thank you for the safety and solace your support has provided over the years. Your feedback, faith, and friendship have fueled this book.

I am also grateful to all of my clients who fight so valiantly to overcome disordered eating and negative body image struggles. You inspire, challenge, and teach me how to live authentically every single day. Thank you.

—Carrie Thiel

Special Thanks

For her poetry:

Claire Bachofner is a mother, wife, writer, and a survivor of an eating disorder. Writing poetry has allowed Claire to discover and express the meaning, beauty, and power flowing through all of her life experiences. She has also written longer pieces, some of which have been published in *Mamalode* magazine. Claire enjoys reading, playing with her little girls, drinking coffee, and sleeping. She is grateful for the love and grace in her life.

For her photographs:

Anne Crandall Campbell is a truly gifted photographer and outdoor adventurer. She helps others discover nature through her business, Wholesome Adventures. Anne's photos capture nature's awesome beauty allowing her to share it with people as though it were a gift to their souls. She is also the best mom imaginable to four incredible children.

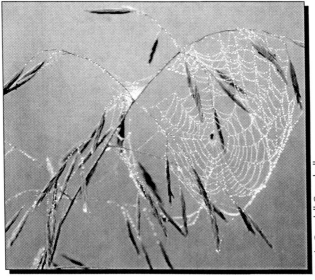

Annie Crandall Campbell

Contents

Introduction

Why a Book by a Therapist and a Mentor

Recovery from an eating disorder is difficult work, no matter how motivated you are to regain health. Traditionally, eating disorder treatment teams have included medical experts, dieticians/nutritionists, and therapists. Recently, some treatment teams are also including mentorship from an eating disorder survivor, similar to the Alcoholics Anonymous model of sponsorship for a person gaining sobriety.

We—Barbi Webber, eating disorder survivor and mentor, and Carrie Thiel, licensed clinical professional counselor—have officially been working together on behalf of our clients for over three years. Previous to that, we worked together in school settings (where Carrie was a teacher) and with parents (when Carrie's daughter was in recovery). You'll learn more about each of us as you read on. We have found that our professional collaboration in support of our clients' health has brought benefits for them, and for us.

In their work with Carrie, clients begin to understand the unique forces at work in their lives and minds that produced disordered eating and/or distorted body image. Using the insights they gain from therapy, they are able to make more positive choices and regain health. Barbi shares with clients how to navigate the day-to-day struggles that come with incorporating healthy eating and body behaviors back into their lives. Because she has *lived it*, Barbi serves as a role model for recovery, sharing the tips, tricks, tools, and strategies that have helped her and others along the way.

Any professional who has assisted eating disordered clients knows the work can be difficult and frustrating, as well as rewarding and enriching. Our professional partnership has allowed us to support not only our clients, but also each other as we face the emotions and challenges inherent in this important work. We brainstorm, commiserate, and celebrate as we engage with each other for our clients' benefit.

Because this partnership has been so advantageous to our clients and us, we wanted to compile what we have learned into one book that clients, concerned family and friends, teachers, coaches, and professionals could use and share with others. As we tell our clients when we suggest tools and strategies to help them: try the ideas in this book that resonate with you. If they are helpful, continue to use them. If not, either adjust them to meet your needs, or discard them from your personal toolbox. All the suggestions in this book are offered with open, hopeful hearts that they can somehow help you find your way back to health. Use them as you see fit.

Poems of Healing, Poems of Life

Throughout this book, you will see poems by Claire Bachofner, an eating disorder survivor of over 12 years. Some poems were written when she was in high school and first dealing with disordered eating and the chaos it brought to her life. Some, expressing more varied themes and emotions, were written later when her recovery was more solid and her life more full.

Claire believes that the act of writing—the deep concentration, the inner search for the right words, the beauty of an original metaphor—helped her heal and keeps her soul alive and strong. She encourages anyone working on becoming more honest and inwardly attuned to experiment with some type of artistic expression. She believes it is essential to recovery.

Claire is Carrie's daughter. When she was first healing from disordered eating, she benefited greatly from working with Barbi. Including Claire's poetry in our book feels like completing a journey that began many years ago. We are so grateful for having come full circle in this collaboration.

Eating Disorder or Disordered Eating?

Eating attitudes and behaviors can be seen as occurring on a continuum with anorexia nervosa on one end and binge eating disorder on the other. In between these two extremes there is an array of chronic or single-episode disordered eating experiences, along with mostly normal eating experiences. If you occasionally ignore your body's natural hunger and satiety cues, like most people in this culture, you fall somewhere in the middle of the eating spectrum. If you ignore these built-in regulation cues on a regular basis, and have some very specific diagnostic symptoms, you may indeed have an eating disorder. A mental health and/or a medical professional should be consulted for an accurate diagnosis if you suspect you or someone else has an eating disorder.

People with eating disorders require and deserve professional treatment to recover. Those who occasionally eat in a disordered fashion may also benefit from consulting a professional, because even without meeting strict diagnostic criteria, disordered eating can impact a person's sense of well-being and enjoyment of life. Also, it can be hard to tell which category you fall into: disordered eating or eating disorder. A professional can help distinguish where you are on the continuum and help you make a plan to deal with it.

Since you are reading this book, you are likely struggling with disordered eating (or someone you love is). Or, perhaps you are educating yourself because you want to be able to offer resources to people about eating disorder recovery. Whatever your reason, we are glad you are seeking help, but please know that this book alone cannot substitute for professional treatment. If you aren't sure where to look for treatment, please see the resources section at the end of the book.

This Substance That Is Me

I carry this body around,
step by step,
breath by breath,
striving to be free.
Bulging with this substance,
this substance that is me.

A container made of elements.
How can that be?
A soul built by experience:
my substance contains me.

Perhaps my aspects bind together
to form a concrete bond
and put me in a state of solid,
too heavy to move on.

Or maybe the elements are more giving,
leaving room to grow—
shuffling, drifting on and on
a delightful liquid flow.

Could it be that I have no boundaries
and my substance is set aflight?
Moving with the grace of air,
this self is but a kite.

True substance is intangible,
and pours me full of fright,
I'll never stop searching
for the substance that feels right.

My body carries me around,
moment by moment,
dream by dream,
striving to be me,
exploding with this substance,
this substance that is me.

—Claire Bachofner

Prologue: The Journey Begins…

Barbi's Story of Surviving Anorexia and Bulimia

What happened? How did a sweet 16-year-old with what seemed like a nearly perfect life ever choose to spiral down into starving, bingeing, and purging her teen years away?

Thirty years later, I continue to ask myself this question.

My motto, "One bite at a time," reveals the answer.

I am now a mentor to others suffering from anorexia, bulimia, binge eating, and many other destructive forms of disordered eating. As I share the tools I used to dig my way out of the deep hole of eating disorder numbness, I gain better understanding of the issues and circumstances that dragged me down. Many of the hopeless feelings I experienced as a sensitive teenager still exist today in other hurting hearts. I care so much as I look into their eyes, and I truly mean it when I say: "I understand how you feel when you torture your body by starving, bingeing, and purging. Walk beside me, and I'll show you a way out."

I mean, really, eating food is fun! How many of us would choose to starve? Think about it: Why would a person make herself or himself throw up many times a day and night? Most of us dread even the yearly flu bug that often causes throw-up episodes. Yuck, we say. It's awfully embarrassing to admit that I chose to make myself throw up my food, and even more embarrassing to have shared it with an audience my very own children were sitting in. But I speak publically now, unafraid to share my story in hopes of helping someone—many people—better understand their eating disorders. For now, if you are one of those people, I want you to know you are not alone. I want to share the parts of my environmental and emotional experiences that took place during the downward spiral of events that almost made me self-destruct.

My family has lived in Duluth, Minnesota, for more than 100 years. I spent my first 15 years in an overloving family consisting of Mom, Dad, two sisters, and a brother, plus lots of Labrador retrievers. My siblings are 12, 10, and 8 years older than I, and with all those older siblings, I felt I actually had four sets of parents! That added up to an overwhelming amount of nurturing. I was never allowed to fall down, make mistakes, and put my pieces together again on my own. My dad owned and operated a beautiful jewelry, china, and gift store on Main Street that has been in our family for nearly 130 years. Lots of social expectations dictated how I dressed and behaved. I could feel the gossip, social judging, and criticism swirling around me. My mother was very involved in the community, was a volunteer-supreme, and the world's finest "helicopter mom." If I ever found myself in a jam, she would swoop down immediately to rescue me.

But honestly, in the midst of this seemingly perfect world, I discovered that life with a severely alcoholic father could be very painful. Especially when all of us "stuffed it" and felt we had to be perfect. We didn't dare show how we felt or what we feared when Dad was drunk—what would people think if they knew? Would our family fall apart? We tried our best to keep things "normal" and preserve our self-image of the perfect family.

In the mid-1970s, I was an active teen who loved sports and was the city champion in speed skating. This was just before women's hockey became popular. Dad was a hockey coach, and he encouraged me to learn how to skate super fast. I enjoyed the challenge. In addition, I was captain of the ninth-grade cheerleading team; I was accomplished at swimming, track, and tennis, and had lots of friends. People said I was pretty. I had boyfriends, too. Summers were filled with canoe camps, fly-fishing trips, and cabins on Minnesota lakes. It seemed like I had it all.

High school was just around the corner. Mom and Dad offered me the privilege of attending an all-female prep school in Connecticut. Also, some Olympic speed skating recruiters visited our home to ask my parents and me to participate in a training program for Olympic hopefuls. I chose the prep school option because I wanted to be well-rounded. I was most intrigued by the idea of leaving home at just 15 and traveling out east for high school.

That fall, I boarded the plane, saying goodbye to family, friends, and a life that would never be the same. I felt sad and nervous, but no crying for this girl. My dad had always told me to quit crying or he'd give me something to cry about: a hard spanking.

I arrived at the new school very excited. The campus was beautiful—600 acres of rolling hills covered with abundant fall colors. I quickly lined up with 350 other girls to choose sports and find out roommate assignments, but none of the sports that had made me popular at home were offered here. My options were: soccer, field hockey, or lacrosse. Gosh, I didn't know a thing about any of them! I picked field hockey because at least I knew the word "hockey." A strange feeling grew inside me. I had gone from an athletic champion in my city to being told I was on the "marshmallow team." That didn't sound or feel so appealing.

Next, I went to find out who my roommates were. I ran up the dorm steps to the room I'd been assigned. As I entered my room, two of the most beautiful girls I'd ever seen stared back at me. One was a Norwegian exchange student: blonde hair, crystal blue eyes, and skinny. The other stunningly gorgeous girl was a professional model in magazines—no kidding! In less than 30 seconds, I concluded that I was the ugliest and fattest one of the three of us. Wow, I'd never thought about myself this way before, but it just seemed as though everything that had made me strong-willed and confident at home didn't exist here, and there was no one to rescue me from these painful thoughts and feelings. My self-esteem and body image, combined with my yearning to belong, began spiraling downward toward a place that felt empty and lonely.

So I went on a "diet"—something I had no experience with and didn't know how to do properly. I began starving myself. I allowed myself very few foods. One of my permitted foods was carrots, and I ate tons of them, so many that within a couple of months my skin turned orange. Even the whites of my eyes and the palms of my hands grew truly orange. I lost many pounds. People began referring to me as an orange skeleton. What a way to gain popularity!

My mother's jaw dropped when she saw me get off the plane for Christmas vacation. Quickly, she got me in to see the family doctor. I was diagnosed as having anorexia nervosa, my new claim to fame. This was the last kind of recognition I'd ever dreamed of causing for myself. But I had to cope with my diagnosis and the shame I felt on my own, because no clear treatment for anorexia existed in the late 1970s. Today, my doctor might have put me in the hospital for intensive treatment, both physical and psychological. Instead, he simply told me to stop what I was doing and start eating right again.

After 10 days of vacation I headed back to prep school, almost as if nothing had happened. Oh, except now I had a label: anorexic. Everyone pretended not to stare, but the word "anorexic" spread like wildfire. I felt like a freak, and everyone was pestering me to eat, eat, eat. By then, I had lost the ability to know how to feed myself, and I felt no connection with my body's need for food. I only knew how to starve, binge, and purge my feelings. When I tried to eat, the food made me feel bloated, yucky, and fat, even though I was voraciously hungry. But I began to gorge myself to make everyone leave me alone and stop pushing me to eat. I can't remember making myself throw up for the first time, but the bloated feeling that followed eating quickly drove me to make purging a way of life. Every day and night, I was consumed with plotting a binge-and-purge session.

Before long I was purging everything I ate, whether it was an apple or a whole grocery bag full of food. My friends told me that what I was doing was disgusting—all but one friend, Anne, who would interrupt my vomiting and encourage me to join her on a walk or to play paddle tennis. I thank dear Anne for being a part of saving my life.

All the while I was self-destructing, I still had a mustard seed-sized grain of faith that whispered repeatedly to stop; it told me this behavior was hurting me mentally and physically. A few scary, horrible bulimic experiences occurred in which I almost passed out and thought I had torn open my throat. They frightened me enough to want to change. But I couldn't stop throwing up everything I ate. I felt disconnected from my mind and body. "Help!" my soul cried.

Somehow my faith, along with my friend Anne, stayed with me. I dug deep inside to find enough courage to try changing the harsh habits that had become my way of coping with life. The art room at school began to lure me away from spending all my time plotting my next binge and purge. I yearned to enter this world of art because it was so free of the need for perfection and critical judgments. Whatever I did to the white canvas with my watercolors was exciting and beautiful to me. I retreated to that art room daily and began to heal.

I had to learn all over again how to eat. My body had lost the ability to be comfortable with, and soothed by, food. Anything I ate—even an apple—made me feel bloated and fat. I'd run to the mirror and stare at my abdomen, hating how huge it looked, telling myself I was gross. Redirecting that thinking was very challenging. I began to focus on other body parts like my eyebrows, eyes, ears, and hands, pulling my mind away from my habitual, destructive self-talk about thighs, butt, and tummy. The more I didn't look at and criticize those parts, the more food I could nourish my body with and keep down. I began with an apple and progressed to moderate amounts of food that felt soothing—safe foods that I trusted.

I grew stronger. I had energy for sports, art, dance, and a social life. And I began to like myself again. Suddenly, I had friends—guess I was not acting so freaky. This life was a whole lot more fun and adventuresome. Sure, I endured some setbacks when life threw some stress-filled events my way, but soon I chose never to go back to starving, bingeing, or purging. I chose to learn many more positive coping skills for surviving life stress. I offer them to you in one of the chapters of this book.

I want to express how much it meant to me when I met and fell in love with my best friend and mate of 33 years, Orrin. Three playful years later we married. Soon after, our son, Blake, was born, followed by our daughter, Brie, three years later. These two beautiful, healthy, gifted children have brought endless joy and adventure to our lives. Had I continued to destroy myself with the physical deprivation from my eating disorders, my body might never have been able to heal enough to provide the nutrition needed to create healthy babies. Had my unhealthy choices in my youth prevented us from having a family, it would have been an unbearable burden to my sensitive soul. I am so thankful to have gained back the health I needed. Honestly, I'm lucky to be alive. Both anorexia and bulimia can result in death for some of those consumed by their torture.

Every day, I deal with embarrassing physical consequences from my anorexic and bulimic behaviors. For instance, I have red, spidery little veins across my cheeks. My legs are riddled with varicose veins that ache, all from the pressure of throwing up. My face was puffy and swollen when my bulimia was active. I have tons of facial hair I remove painfully, monthly. My most treasured sign of the body health I regained was the rhythm of my menstrual periods. I know most young women would rather not have to deal with that monthly flow, but to me, each period is a comforting reminder of my precious family.

However, one of the most serious and unexpected health consequences I've suffered have involved my teeth. This is a difficult story to tell, and possibly to read, but it is important that you know the truth about one possible devastating effect of an eating disorder. About five years ago, as I entered my fifties, my teeth began losing their last layer of enamel and rapidly rotting. Painful pits began to appear, tormenting my oral comfort. Smiling felt awful. My dear dentist and I agreed that this developing deterioration was a direct consequence of my choice to participate in the lies and self-destruction of anorexia and bulimia. Thirty plus years later, though I am now healed,

I am getting payback for what I did to myself in the past: starved, binged, and purged away six valuable developmental years of my life.

Stomach acid and very poor nutrition created a need for total reconstruction of my teeth. Had I known what was to come or listened to my heart telling me to stop because I was hurting myself, I may have been spared this traumatic consequence! The rebuilding of my teeth began with over sixty hours of drilling away all my rotting teeth down to nubbins needed for a crown preparation. I had to just lie there and take the pain as my dentist and her technicians made me as comfortable as possible, which was a *huge* task! It felt as though the drill was in my brain many times. I didn't complain, though, as this was *my fault!* I had to deal with it, and have decided to talk about it so maybe someone thinking an eating disorder could relieve their pain and stress will know the honest truth about the consequences and seek professional healing help.

The most challenging moment came when, while waiting for my new teeth to be made in a lab, I had temporary fake teeth on my jack-o-lantern nubbins. They were only meant to be in my mouth a short period of time, and it had been a rough go for them to survive my daily chewing, brushing, grinding, and so forth. I was scheduled to present a mindful eating practice session this particular noon and, after fueling up with some food for energy before the event, I began to remove the retainers I wore to help me eat. Suddenly, my two front teeth *fell out!*

I was to be a motivational speaker in 45 minutes, and the visual I saw in the mirror was mortifying. I knew I had to deal with it, so I brushed up and stuck the teeth back on with my spit. I would have to tell the whole class my challenge and why I couldn't mindfully eat with them that day. We all watched for the teeth to fall out during my presentation, but saliva is a miracle glue! The group was very supportive and caring and enjoyed taking turns sharing tooth-related stress experiences—bonding supreme! I am proud that I didn't freak out and quit by not showing up to face my ordeal and my group. Life dishes it, and this was one of those moments when I had to dig deep and was glad I stepped up in the end.

Honestly, I find it ironic that long ago, when I went down the self-destructive path of eating disorders and negative body image, I was actually trying to achieve body perfection along with overachieving in every area of my teenage life. I didn't like me as myself and viewed me as not good enough anywhere. I felt I needed to be someone different in mind and body presentation in order to be accepted. Did any of the anorexic or bulimic thoughts or behaviors help me achieve these sought after attributes? *No!* Instead, I gradually began to rediscover my authentic self and nourish the realization that this pure me being had always been *more* than good enough. Unfortunately, years later I am experiencing what eating disorders *really* do to people. It is not a matter of *if* you are going to feel the painful consequences; rather, it is *when* you will feel them.

I know some other survivors of anorexia and bulimia who do *not* have their original teeth. No one talks about it. Well, I am going to. Someone needs to speak up and tell the truth to other hurting souls so that they back away from the darkness and lies of eating disorder thinking and behaving that could result in killing their *natural beauty*. Remember: you only get one set of your very own teeth. Please turn your direction toward your positive light and healing so that you can regain your smile and shine in recovery celebration. Please reach out to your dentist for help. It is *never* too late!

I care so much about you, and I pray that you never experience what I have had to endure with my teeth restoration. I have to be honest and out-loud bold in sharing this survival journey.

Back to other aspects of my recovery story, after I earned my bachelor's degree in social work, I knew my life work needed to be helping people in times of suffering. During college, I began supporting and mentoring a few young women who were caught in the grip of bulimia. I've been mentoring frightened young women for the past 30-plus years. I share my journey with them, offering hope and understanding. Faith has provided me the courage to speak out publicly to thousands of people about eating disorder education, awareness, and prevention. I share my personal survival journey into and out of anorexia and bulimia. I can say that I've been there and done that, and I want to spend the rest of my life walking beside others as they leave that hopeless place. I want to encourage their second chance at life, to share hope, health, and healing with others who need a friend as they combat an eating disorder.

I honestly feel deeply blessed to be a motivational mentor working with people who struggle with disordered eating illnesses. I also respect and believe in a team approach to healing, which means working with: mental health therapists, exercise specialists, doctors, nurses, dieticians/nutritionists, and other health professionals, as well as teachers, counselors, social workers, and communities to provide hope and healing for those who have eating disorders. All team members bring the benefits of their knowledge, experience, and individuality to provide a wraparound approach guiding those who suffer toward their own place of health.

If you were in my office right now, we would share a big hug. Let your journey begin!

"You have to travel the healing journey in order to arrive!
May I help inspire your new *appetite for life."*

Carrie's Story: It Runs in Families

When my daughter, Claire, first began to restrict her food intake, I brushed it off as a phase. At 14, she played soccer, excelled in school, had lots of friends, and seemed comfortable in her own skin. Little did I know that under that skin, deep in her heart, she was carrying a heavy burden of emotional distress. Experience, genetics, circumstances, culture, and relationships all came together one summer and overwhelmed her ability to cope. She went on her first diet, and before long became ensnared in the web of disordered eating.

What is more primal than a mother's desire to nourish her child? What could be more devastating than watching your child disappear physically, emotionally, intellectually, pound by pound? How do you withstand the judgment, misunderstanding, and dismissal of eating disorders by family, friends, school, and the culture at large while your child cries herself to sleep and talks of suicide? Eating disorders involve more than the damaging physical and emotional symptoms; they hide behind a cloak of secrecy and shame, leaving sufferers and their loved ones feeling alone in their despair.

For three intense years, Claire journeyed toward health, and today, 14 years later, she is a strong woman—a wife, mother, and writer. At certain times, old, destructive thinking patterns and behaviors have crept back into her life, and when she has realized it, she has faced it and dealt with it. Mostly, she revels in the beautiful life she has created for herself and her family. As her mom, I've walked a path parallel to Claire's, but different. I had to learn the toughest lesson of all for those who love someone with an eating disorder: letting go. Not abandoning, or ignoring, or denying Claire's illness, but letting go of thinking I could fix it. There were things I could do that were helpful to her recovery, and things that could be unhelpful, but ultimately, it was only Claire herself who could make the choice and do the work required to gain health. I am so grateful she chose to become well, and that I learned how to stand strong with her.

How did she make her way back to health? With determination, focus, creativity, patience, endurance, courage, and with the loving help of many, including trained professionals. She received care at an inpatient treatment center, and when she left there, she worked with a psychotherapist, a nurse practitioner, a dietician, and a mentor, my co-author, Barbi Webber. Claire took responsibility for the day-to-day, meal-by-meal work of overcoming disordered eating and thinking, which, in this culture, is hard work. It was not a straight line from treatment to recovery, but more of a spiraling path, where certain lessons had to be learned again and again as she journeyed toward recovery.

Research shows that disordered eating tends to run in families, and that is certainly true in Claire's case. Until now, I have not admitted publically to my own history of disordered eating and negative body image. I have not talked about myself in relation to Claire's story because I didn't want to take the healing spotlight off of her, but now, as a therapist who works with clients with eating disorders, and as a person still working to live out the same healthy lifestyle I encourage in others, it is time to own up to my struggles.

As a child, I was what was called "chubby." Most of the time, I didn't think much of it, but when there were no Brownie Scout uniforms in my size, or I got called names, I felt deeply ashamed. The first time the word "diet" appeared in my diary was when I was 11. It was something I would do on and off for the next several years, but when I was 17, it became a serious problem.

Over the next year, I would diet to cope with fear of life after high school graduation, to heal a broken heart, to bolster my self-esteem, and, ultimately, to avoid making difficult choices about how to grow up, leave home, and start a life of my own, though

I didn't know that was why I was doing it. I thought I was doing it *just* so I would look great, because I had been brainwashed to believe that if you *look* great (according to our cultural standards), you *feel* great! During that year, I received compliments and attention from all sorts of people who had never noticed me before, and it did feel good. How I looked replaced academic achievement as the most worthy goal I could strive for. And, of course, it was reinforced everywhere I looked.

I stopped having my period, became anxious and preoccupied with calorie counting, couldn't focus, and started isolating myself. Nowadays, I'd probably receive a diagnosis of either anorexia nervosa or eating disorder not otherwise specified. But, since it was the late 1970s, no one said anything about my extreme dieting being problematic.

Over the next 30 years, I never went back to the severe food restriction I followed during my teen years, but I also didn't make peace with normal eating or the way my body looked. I joined the millions of women in this culture who believe they'd feel and look so much better if they could just lose 10 to 15 pounds, which kept me always a little anxious and unable to appreciate the good health and strong body I did have.

It wasn't until Claire's diagnosis of anorexia that I had to reconsider everything I'd ever believed about food, dieting, body image, self-esteem, health, and femininity in this culture. These are things I still wrestle with, albeit in much more honest, loving, healthful ways. Watching Claire and the women I work with each day look honestly at themselves, their families, their cultures, their fears, their hopes, and their dreams has inspired me to do the same. I am grateful for what Claire's struggle and recovery taught me, even while I would give anything for her not to have gone through it.

It was during Claire's journey that I first met Barbi. She led an eating disorder support group at Claire's high school. Claire told me Barbi's advice and encouragement were extremely helpful to her. When I asked her how they helped, she said that Barbi gave the girls very specific ideas and strategies for dealing with very specific eating and body image issues, such as brushing her teeth right after she ate to help her mind shift from an eating event to the next part of her life. It provided a ritual, if you will, to signal to the brain: mealtime is over, so let it go and get on with your life. This may sound simple, but for someone struggling to regain normal behavior around food, it felt like a revelation! Plus, Claire said, Barbi had lived her recovery for over 20 years, was a mom and wife, and a nice, caring person who gave Claire and the other girls hope that they, too, could overcome their disordered eating and live happy lives.

Knowing this had been Claire's experience with Barbi, I invited her to come speak to a support group I had started for parents whose children had eating disorders. Her kind, but frank, information and discussion helped us better understand our children's struggles and how we could support them. I've worked with Barbi many times since then, most recently on this book, and I value the insight, hope, and tools she offers to those with disordered eating.

As years passed and Claire grew healthier, I realized that my "hobby" of eating disorder education, support, and advocacy was pulling my attention and energy toward the idea of a new career. I decided to leave teaching and become a professional counselor. Now, five years into this new work, I am honored to support those struggling with all kinds of emotional and life issues, and most certainly that includes people experiencing disordered eating. I believe professional counseling is critical to eating disorder recovery, as is a wide network of support in one's community.

Fortunately, Barbi continues to work as a mentor through a structured program called Body Balance. Many of my clients have worked with her and vice versa. In counseling, people work hard to resolve the deeper issues underlying their disordered eating. In a mentoring relationship, they learn helpful cognitive behavioral tools that Barbi has developed over the years. I am grateful for the complementary, supportive work we do with people, and the positive effect I've seen it have.

To be able to share my experiences in this book, to have Claire contribute her poetry, and to help Barbi share her story and tools has been a work of love and appreciation. I hope that those who read this book find hope, healing, and practical methods for themselves, those they love, and those they may work with on a professional basis.

Thin

I remember that one pair of
doll-sized gray pants that
flared at the ankles.
Zipped up the back,
and caught everyone's eye.

I remember thousands of to-go cups
filled with bitter, hot, strong,
black coffee.
The perfect high-energy
low-calorie beverage
for a girl on the move.

I remember all the times
I watched my classmates
fade to broken pixels
as my vision went black,
and my neck tensed,
and I would have to find my way
to the drinking fountain.
Ears ringing,
knees giving,
I'd gulp down enough water
to keep burning energy upon the
excessively waxed floorboards of the high school gymnasium.

I remember shivering,
and shuddering,
with blue hands
and a pale face,
taking breaths more shallow than mud puddles,
and thinking it was all so worth it,
until it wasn't.

Until the tears stung and swelled my eyes
and I found myself signing stacks of papers
and watching my mother's spirit collapse
as she left her daughter
nine hours from home,
on the third floor of an old brick building,
terrified.

Until I was standing,
frozen, sobbing, starving,
in Exam 1.
With a needle in my skin
and fear rushing through my veins.
My pleading eyes met
the nurse's blank stare,
and I realized the worst was yet to come:
Tonight,
they'd make me eat.

—Claire Bachofner

In recovering from disordered eating, you will spend time with a therapist to understand the psychology behind why you have developed disordered eating and how to make positive changes to overcome it. You will also work with a medical professional to address the serious physical aspects of eating disorders. With a nutritionist or dietician, you will learn the facts about food so you can make the best nutritional choices possible as you seek health. If you are lucky enough to work with a recovery mentor, you will also likely learn some very practical methods for coping with day-to-day life, which can be tremendously helpful in navigating the tricky path out of disordered eating. If you do not have a mentor to work with, hopefully, you can experiment with the ideas in this chapter, which have been developed by a mentor, and which many people have found helpful, especially when used in conjunction with conventional therapy.

These ideas are the heart and soul of this book. They are designed to be healthy and soothing to your mind, body, and spirit and to help you cope with life stress. Many of them deserve a more expansive discussion, so you'll read about those in more depth in later chapters. Please keep an experimental and curious attitude as you consider these tools, and try them out in your own life. Some will feel perfect for you; some will not. You can always modify them to fit your own circumstances, style, and goals. There is no right or wrong approach, so don't let any perfectionist tendencies keep you from trying some of these ideas and making them work for you.

The tools are arranged under headings that suggest what area of eating disorder recovery they address. Even though some strategies address multiple recovery topics, they are only mentioned one time under the heading that seems to be the best fit. Please remember that it is you, the reader, who will figure out, through trial and correction, whether or not a tool works for you and how, and that is just as it should be.

Along with these cognitive behavioral skills, you will find stories from Barbi's personal life as an eating disorder survivor, and her professional life as a motivational mentor. Hopefully, they will help you understand how these tools play out in the lives of real people who use them, and give you ideas about how you might make them work for you.

Your body has a voice. Learn to listen to it. Heal from the inside out. Practice these strategies. Persevere—one bite at a time.

Mindful Awareness

One of the hallmarks of disordered eating is eating while distracted, or eating to numb difficult or intense emotions. Eating is transformed from a physiological necessity rich with cultural and social meaning to a psychological coping mechanism with many negative side effects, including mindlessness.

The most powerful way to get out of the mindless eating trap is to start paying attention to what, when, where, why, and how you eat. Mindful eating is a skill you can relearn. Following are some strategies to help you do so. Some of them involve food, and some of them do not, but the awareness you gain from any one of them will help with mindful eating. An entire chapter is dedicated to this concept later in the book.

Mindful Bites

Mindful eating might very well be the most important skill presented in this book. It will allow you to remember the purpose and meaning of eating: to nourish your body so that you can live your life.

Disordered eaters can get so lost in their fear and worries about food, or in the numbing out trance induced by bingeing, that they forget all they were born knowing about how to eat: eat when you're hungry and stop when you are satisfied. Relearning your innate sense of how to eat requires that you slow down, notice what you're eating, notice how it feels in your body, and take special care to calm any anxieties or worries that arise.

Following is how it is done:
- Gather your food.
- Take a moment to be grateful; think of something positive in your life.
- Have one to three bites of your food.
- Put your food and utensils down.
- Touch your napkin to calm anxiety.
- Take a sip of liquid; let it soothe you.
- Breathe more than once.
- Check in to see if you are stressed.
- If you feel stressed, take some more deep breaths and tell the stress it is *not* invited to this meal.
- Tune in to your body's deep awareness of its needs: are you hungry, satisfied, or full?
- Turn your attention to a card or uplifting picture, if you are alone.
- In a social eating setting, express the need for kind conversation if topics turn negative.
- Enjoy more bites!
- Repeat, repeat, and repeat this mindful eating rhythm.

Mindful bites helped me to slow down and stopped my disordered eating behaviors. I learned how to enjoy eating again as I healed from anorexia and bulimia. Mindful bites saved my life over and over.

The Power of Positive Self-Talk While Eating

It is necessary to replace the negative self-talk of disordered eating with positive thoughts. What you think affects how you feel emotionally, and how you feel emotionally affects what you *do*—your actions. This is why it is so important to tune in to your inner dialogue. Notice the negative judgments and harsh thoughts regarding food and your body that arise when you are eating. Choose to change those thoughts so that you can nourish yourself well.

Repeat to yourself: "This food is good for me. This will not hurt me. I can trust this food to nourish my body and keep me alive. I am making the healthy, life-sustaining choice by eating."

Give yourself permission to eat.

Stop and Enjoy the Moment

It can be so easy to rush through our work, your play time, your family time, and your meals. What is the rush? Life is not a race, and it can truly only be lived one moment at a time. If you want to learn to nurture yourself and nourish your body, you will need to learn to stop and enjoy the moments in your day, one at a time. Tune into your senses: notice what you see, hear, feel, smell, and taste, and just linger in that moment. Then, move on. Research is showing, more and more, the benefits of stopping to enjoy the moment.

Self-Care

What is meant by the term *self-care*? Self-care refers to all the things you do to nurture, nourish, and care for yourself in order to create and maintain good health. Effective self-care creates a sense of well-being in mind, body, and spirit, which will support your recovery from disordered eating. Another important result is so that you are well and energized and can care lovingly for the important people and things in your life.

For some reason, many people with eating disordered habits have learned to place everyone else's care and needs ahead of their own, and then they end up depleted of energy, health, and peace. This empty, tired feeling can send them into disordered eating thinking and behaviors, hoping to feel replenished by them. Instead, they feel more drained. If this sounds like you, then it is time to put into place a good self-care routine. Doing so will actually allow you to be more effective in helping others because you'll feel better yourself.

Some ideas you might want to try as part of your personal self-care plan include the following:
- Walking or other moderate exercise, with doctor's approval, if necessary
- Eating nutritious foods at regular intervals, as prescribed by your dietician or nutritionist
- Enjoying a professional massage once in a while

- Caring lovingly for your appearance—haircuts, manicures, spa time (at home, if you can't afford to pay a professional)
- Creative time: writing, painting, knitting, sewing, making collages, photography, other hobbies, visiting art galleries or museums or antique stores
- Social time with special, positive, supportive friends
- Spiritual time: reading, meditating, praying, attending religious services, time in nature

Some ideas you might want to try as part of your personal self-care plan include creative time such as photography.

You might be able to think of many more activities that energize you and help you feel good.

In order to make sure that self-care activities happen, write or program them into your daily planner. Whenever someone needs you during your planned self-care time, advocate for your wellness by letting others know you are not available then, but are willing to help at another time. You can also think of yourself as a role model, showing others that it is okay and healthy to take care of yourself.

Tips for Staying Centered

Life will bring you many joys, and many sorrows, and many things in between. There is no way around this fact, even though many people resist it, wishing for nothing but joy, and then feeling let down and disappointed when they have to deal with difficulties.

Once you accept that your life will contain a mixture of good and bad, easy and hard, light and dark, then you can deal with stressful events more successfully, and without turning to disordered eating behavior.

Following is a quick list of simple ideas and concepts that you might ponder, journal about, or post somewhere to remind you of how to move through your day with more emotional ease:

- Don't worry so much. Nothing that has (or has not) happened has been due to worry.
- Try not to be so fearful. Trust that you can handle the events of your life.
- Move through life transitions or difficult tasks one step at a time.
- Realize that problems will come and go, so don't linger on them.
- Pay attention to your health needs, and let go of other people's problems.
- Count your blessings—don't overlook even the smallest. Gratitude is healing.
- Listen to your whole body's need for nourishment of mind, body, and spirit.
- Learn to "God bless it" and let it go, let it go, and let it go some more by turning worries over to whatever higher power you trust in: God, nature, fate, the universe, or the like.

Worry, worry, worry—where does that get you? Nowhere! Why worry about tomorrow? There is enough worry in today, and none of it belongs in your nourishment routine. Don't let a decision that will come due in two months affect whether you eat healthfully today. Feed and hydrate yourself *today* in order to be healthy and strong for all the tomorrows to come. Take worries to your counselor and seek to understand them more deeply as well as to explore new ways to cope with them, or let them go.

Food and Food Preparation

Anything having to do with food or food preparation can be very challenging for a person with disordered eating. A person who has a problem with drugs or alcohol can choose to avoid being around those substances and the places they are sold. Yes, it is extremely hard for them to do so, but they can make that choice. For a person recovering from disordered eating, the choice to never be around food again is simply not an option. In fact, recovery *requires* that you be around food, but with a more mindful, peaceful attitude.

Anything having to do with food or food preparation can be very challenging for a person with disordered eating. Recovery requires that you be around food, but with a more mindful, peaceful attitude.

The tools and strategies in this section are suggested to help you find a more creative and balanced approach towards eating and food preparation. Read them over, experiment with them, and make them your own.

Boundary Plates

If you feel anxious eating or serving from a large plate, find some pretty dishes, cups, and bowls in sizes appropriate for the portions you need to eat. This can help if you have gotten in the habit of truly eating more than your body needs and you feel too full. Or, if you're not used to eating enough, different sized dishes can help you know that you are. Using "kinder" dishes can help you know for sure you're eating enough in proper proportions, according to your particular dietary needs, as set out by your nutritionist or dietician.

Cooler and Food Bag

Planning ahead for your nutritional needs is one way to keep yourself in recovery mode. Sometimes, you will have to eat away from home, and doing so can evoke anxiety, which can make you turn to your old habits just to get through a worrisome time.

Instead of resorting to automatic disordered eating behaviors because you're not at home, buy a cooler that will fit easily into your car. In it, you can place portioned amounts of food that fit with your dietary needs. Also, get a sturdy bag to carry the food you will need for meals and snacks at work, school, or while traveling. Between your cooler and food bag, you will be ready to enjoy worry-free, safe, trusted, on-the-go food wherever you are.

Tidy the Kitchen Before Eating

For many people who struggle with mindless, out-of-control eating, tidying up the kitchen after a meal or food preparation time can pose a challenge. What follows is a way to make the post-meal time more peaceful.

Prepare your meal, and place it at your table setting. Go back into the kitchen. Put away all counter foods. Cover and refrigerate leftovers. Sit and enjoy your food. After your meal, clean your dishes, and move on to the next activity in your life.

It's Okay to Throw It Away

Many people eat beyond their body's fullness cues because of a belief that it is not okay to throw food away when there are people in this world who go hungry. While this may seem like a logical belief, it actually doesn't make any sense at all. Whether or not you end a meal with a clean plate does nothing for a person somewhere in the world who doesn't have enough food. Instead, it keeps you locked into disordered eating behaviors. If you truly are concerned about helping people who don't have enough to eat, then get involved in an organization that works to feed the hungry, but when it comes to your own food intake, try the following ideas to let go of food you don't need to satisfy *your* body's needs.

During mealtimes, be sure to eat while listening closely to your hunger, satiety, and fullness cues. If you have eaten mindfully, and find that you have truly had enough, but there is still some food on your plate, please remember: you *don't* need to be a member of the clean-plate club if your body is telling you something different. You can either throw the food away, or put it in a container to save for another meal, if that is a safe recovery behavior for you. Either way, you *do not have to eat it*!

Honestly look in your refrigerator and cupboards for foods that are not contributing to your healing efforts. Take these foods, and either give or throw them away. Be sure to demolish the thrown-away foods by squishing them into the garbage. This way you won't be tempted to dig them back out if you doubt that you did the right thing, or if the urge to binge on them comes back later.

If anorexia or not eating enough has been your main struggle, *do not use this tool as an excuse to get rid of the food you need to eat to regain health*! Be honest with yourself as you choose which food you need and/or should keep in your home, in consultation with your dietician.

The Treat Egg

Recovering from disordered eating doesn't mean giving up any foods that you love; in fact, it is quite the opposite: it means realizing you can eat all foods, in the right proportion, by listening to your body and mindfully eating proper proportions for your body's needs. That includes treats—whatever yours may be!

One idea for being mindful about how much of a treat you eat is to put it into one of those plastic Easter eggs. Fill the egg with a treat of your choosing and enjoy eating it mindfully when you feel hungry for it.

Be sure to time the use of this strategy so that it feels comfortable with your level of recovery. For some, even a small treat doesn't yet feel comfortable. When you are ready, and with the support of your treatment team, this could be a fun tool for you to experiment with.

The point is that you don't have to go without—restriction and deprivation are part of your old disordered eating mindset. With the treat egg, you're in charge!

The Beauty of the Tray

Creating healthy boundaries in your life means you have thoughtfully discerned when to say yes, and when to say no. This can be applied to all aspects of your life: relationships, career, social life, and finances. For people with a history of disordered eating, this can also include the topics of food, exercise, and healthy thoughts. Sometimes, a visual cue can help you make the best choice about what to eat and how much, while you are still learning to respond mindfully to your body's hunger cues. Following is an idea to try: Take a TV or serving tray and load it with your meal choices, all placed in appropriate serving sized dishes. You can have enjoyment of the food you desire while having the sanctuary of a boundary you can see.

Take a TV or serving tray and load it with your meal choices, all placed in appropriate serving sized dishes. You can have enjoyment of the food you desire while having the sanctuary of a boundary you can see.

User-Friendly Food

Work with your dietician to develop an array of foods you can eat with absolutely no fears—foods you can choose to nurture your mind, body, and spirit anytime, day or night. Rely on these foods during any setbacks or stressful times, when dealing with new foods might feel like too much. Don't allow the eating disorder to be a saboteur in your healing progress by creating anxiety over unfamiliar foods that scare you and keep you from eating. Do what you need to do in order to keep the nourishment coming.

Cook for Others

While food, at its most basic, nourishes your physical body, it also serves an important social function. Sharing food and meals is one way people connect with each other. Preparing food that you enjoy for those you love—when you are ready—can help you strengthen relationships and remind you of *why* you want to recover: to have more energy to enjoy your life and those you love! Cooking might even become a creative outlet and meaningful social activity for you. It could become a new kind, healthy food habit. Don't forget to enjoy, with your loved ones, the food you so lovingly create.

Delicious Sounds

Try making joyful noises when you eat. Food tastes so good, and you've worked so hard to relearn how to enjoy each bite. Let your mind, body, and spirit rejoice that you no longer starve, binge, or purge. Say out loud: "This is delicious!" or "Yum!" or "How tasty!" Don't hold back; give voice to the delight of nourishing your whole self.

Soothing, Comforting, Centering

Many people develop disordered eating in an attempt to relieve the stress and anxiety they feel brought about by difficult events, people, or situations in their lives. Unfortunately, this very natural attempt to try to feel better eventually backfires, leaving people feeling more stressed and anxious than ever.

There are many, many ways you can learn to truly soothe and comfort yourself that have no negative side effects. In fact, if you practice these strategies, you may find yourself feeling more centered and balanced in many areas of your life. The positive side effects are many, but one of the best is experiencing restored emotional, physical, and spiritual wellness.

Rebalance Kit

I love to use my rebalance kit items for a peaceful, nourishing, and calming transition from eating to other activities in my life. When I began to use this kit, I realized that it stopped me from turning my eating experience into a binge/purge episode that left me depleted and filled with guilt and shame. My rebalance kit rescued me and set me on a path to a binge/purge-free life.

A rebalance kit is a collection of nurturing items that will help you practice self-soothing in positive ways instead of turning to disordered eating behaviors. You can use your kit anytime you feel anxious and/or to help you transition to and from eating times. In fact, make more than one so you have one with you all the time, wherever and whenever you need one. You could keep one in your car, locker, purse, backpack, office drawer, bedside table, kitchen, living room, or other helpful places.

Choose a bag that you will fill with your kit items. It could be plain or fancy, cloth or paper—whatever appeals to *you*! Find soothing things that nurture your senses yet are *not* food, such as: a picture of people that love you and that you love, essential oils, perfume, hand sanitizer, hair brush, nail file, book of quotes, paintbrush, markers, paper, gum, mints, lip balm, lotion, toothbrush and paste, mouthwash, dental floss, aromatherapy items, nail polish, and so forth. Enjoy being creative by selecting items that really appeal to you

No-Binge-Eating Zone

Sometimes it can be helpful to set real physical boundaries around yourself to help reinforce the emotional boundaries you are trying to create with food. The no-binge-eating zone is a strategy to do just that.

Select or create a place, such as a favorite chair or a special rug, where you will never allow binge eating. Move to it when you feel urges to binge eat. Collect your thoughts; use positive self-talk to remind yourself of your health goals and the reasons you want to heal. Use a rebalance kit, read from an inspirational book, listen to some soothing music, take some deep relaxing breaths, roll your shoulders, and get centered. When you feel calmer, stronger, and ready to move on to other things, do so, and feel proud that you defeated disordered eating.

Jupiterimages/Photos.com/Thinkstock

Select or create a place, such as a favorite chair, where you will never allow binge eating. Move to it when you feel urges to binge eat.

I have one of my grandma's old-fashioned cookie tins that I turned into a treasure tin and filled with items that bring me memories of delight: heart rocks, angel figurines, sea glass, jasmine soap, bird nest yarn, faith writings, lavender sachet, paint brush, cards from loved ones. My treasure tin sits next to my no-snack zone chair and is waiting for me to connect whenever I need to remind myself that I am not missing out on the joys of life by thinking negatively, but instead, I will engage in life's positivity.

Soothing After a Meal

You need to focus on soothing thoughts and behaviors as you transition from eating to the next part of your day or night without succumbing to the negative thoughts and behaviors that used to rule your life. How do you do that? Following are some ideas:

- Activate your rebalance kit.
- Lie down on your back or side to take the pressure off your fullness.
- Breathe; realize the food you ate is now refueling your mind, body, and spirit.
- Keep negative, sabotaging thoughts away. If they arise, gently bring your thoughts back to positive, healing thoughts.
- Tuck a pillow between your legs as you breathe deeply and relax into the moment.
- Resume life and living.
- Feel proud.

Nurture Your Sense of Touch

Many people experience comfort and relaxation by touching soft cuddly items, like: a blanket, sweater, yarn, silky material, ribbon, or such. You might find that running your hands or fingers over soft, silky things really soothes you and helps relieve anxious thoughts and feelings. Be willing to experiment by visiting a fabric store, craft store, or your own closets to look for things to which your unique sense of touch favorably responds.

Bathing Beauty

Many people enjoy the comforting experience of a luxurious bath. The warm, soothing water drains away stress and can bring mind, body, and spirit back into balance. The act of bathing—and the bathtub—can become a refuge for a tired, anxious body to become refreshed.

*Many people enjoy the comforting experience of a
luxurious bath. The warm, soothing water drains away stress
and can bring mind, body, and spirit back into balance.*

As you enter the water, tune your brain to mindful positive thoughts. Focus on what has gone well recently. Then, invite more of your senses into the moment. Enjoy the light and scent of a candle. Feel the soft warm water on your skin. Turn on some relaxing music or enjoy the quiet. Relax. Breathe deeply. Let go of worry. Enjoy the beauty of bathing!

Body and Body Image

One of the most difficult aspects of healing from disordered eating may be developing positive feelings about your body and its appearance. The normal, healthy connection between mind and body can be lost when you become so focused on calories in and out. The stress that develops, or that was there to begin with, interrupts your body's inherent communication system, and can result in feelings of dissatisfaction, disgust, or even hatred. Trying to heal a body toward which you feel hate and anger will not work. Love is what you need to cultivate as you consider your body, all it does for you, and yes, even how it looks. With a kind, compassionate, supportive attitude and perspective toward your whole self—including your body—you will be able to respect and appreciate it more fully, and want to care for it.

An important concept to put into practice is to stop trying to be something that your gene pool would never create. One of the things that led me to anorexia and bulimia was that I became very tall, very young, just like one of my grandmas, who was 5 feet, 10 inches. Instead of accepting this fact about myself, I decided I wanted to be petite. I think I may have completely self-destructed with anorexia trying to become something my body was incapable of being. I encourage you to become friendly with your genes.

Following are some ideas, exercises, strategies, and tools to help you repair negative body image and create a positive, loving attitude toward your body.

Body Distortion

Sometimes, you truly cannot see yourself for real. You look in the mirror, and all you can focus on are "fat" thighs, bottom, abdomen, and such. This can be true no matter what your real size is—all you can see is a reflection that you don't like or want. One way to begin to change this habit of looking for what you don't like is to make a decision to find something to like about your appearance, and then to make that decision a daily habit.

You might scan your face, your head, your arms and legs, your toes and fingers—anywhere—in search of an area or part of your body that you can at least accept, just as it is. Each day, go back to that place on your body, acknowledge that you like it and see if you can increase your acceptance of it. It may feel funny, or not entirely sincere, at first, but given time, you really can learn to appreciate aspects of your appearance. Once this appreciation becomes more automatic, scan around for another area of your body or appearance that you can begin to accept and love. Whenever you look in a mirror, go to those areas first and last, so you can begin and end with a loving attitude.

Photograph Me

Have someone you trust take some pictures of you so that you can see yourself honestly. When you see the images, focus on the areas of your appearance that you appreciate and let go of looking at any part of your body that causes negative feelings. If it is too difficult to do that right now, then don't do it, but consider it a goal for further along in your recovery.

Feel-Good Pants

Bodies—especially women's bodies—can vary in how they feel and look over the course of a week, a month, a year, or a lifetime. Rather than cultivate feelings of anger and frustration about these inevitable changes, try learning to accommodate them with more accepting attitude and actions.

Sort through your wardrobe, and try to find five pairs of pants that will feel comfortable on your body during its different stages of change. Some pairs will be looser and some will be tighter as your body moves through its normal cycles. By having these different sizes of pants available, you can learn to like how you feel and look all month long, not just on a day or two. Some people cut the size tags out of their clothes as soon as they bring them home so that they can choose based on comfort of their bodies, not on what size the pants are.

You deserve to be comfortable. You deserve to look nice. Prepare your wardrobe so that you can.

Put Your Jeans Back On

The day after you have eaten what feels to you like too much or a lot, try putting your favorite jeans back on. Sometimes people avoid this because they are afraid the pants won't fit, thinking they've gained 20 pounds in one day. Instead of staying in that negative, fearful mindset, which can lead to making other negative, destructive choices, just go put your pants on and face the truth. Then, make the next most loving choice for how to treat your body and move on.

Scarves

A simple and inexpensive way to brighten your appearance, regardless of your size, is to use a pretty scarf as a stylish accessory. Scarves allow you to play with color, pattern, and texture and can help you look more polished. This can help boost your confidence in your appearance so that you can move through your day with a more positive attitude.

Reflection Talk

Mirrors can be tools for recovery or sabotage, depending upon your attitude when you look in one. You can focus on what you perceive to be the negative and set yourself up to turn to disordered eating behaviors, hoping they'll change your perceptions. Or, you can choose to gaze at yourself with a different mindset, and loosen negative body image's hold on your emotions and actions.

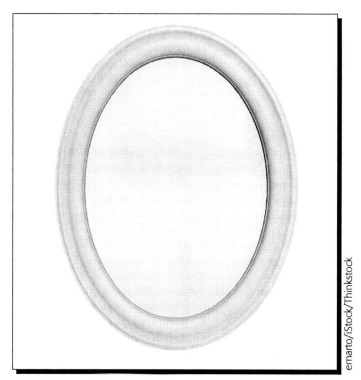

Mirrors can be tools for recovery or sabotage,
depending upon your attitude when you look in one.

Whenever you look at your reflection in a mirror or window, try saying one of these kind expressions to yourself, or out loud:

- *"Okay, fine!"* This phrase can help signify to yourself that you are okay, you are fine, and you are moving forward in your life regardless of what you see in the mirror. If you catch an unexpected glimpse of yourself in a mirror or other reflective surface and it surprises you in an uncomfortable way, use this phrase to move forward in your day and let it go.
- *"Good to go!"* This phrase is something you can think to yourself when you need to check to see that your clothes are clean and straightened, hair is fixed, face is washed, and teeth are clean. It is a statement of gentle appraisal and acceptance and tells you that you are ready to face the event, the day, and the life that is waiting for you.

Clothes That Fit

As your body heals, it will likely shift its shape, perhaps several times. Many people say that it feels strange to watch and experience these changes, even though they signify increasing health. This means you will likely need to acquire new clothing. The answer? Go shopping!

If you don't have much of a budget for clothing, try thrift stores. They have many fun choices and styles. Even if you feel afraid to do so, get clothes that fit your body *now*, and don't look back. By all means, get rid of the old clothes because they are not *supposed* to fit anymore. The person they fit before was *dying* from disordered eating and its deadly grasp. The sooner you get rid of the past and the clothes that represent the sickness and danger of it, the sooner you will be able to embrace and celebrate the new you!

One thing that can be hard about shopping is trying on clothes in front of the mirror. It can be helpful to do some deep breathing and use self-talk to remind you of why you are there: to buy clothes that fit and that you like, in some way—color, texture, fit, and so forth. Some people face away from the mirror as they slip in and out of clothes, only turning around once they have an outfit completely on. They do not linger on looking at parts of their bodies that cause them distress; they focus on the outfit: Does it fit? Do I like it? Am I going to buy it? They, then turn back around, change, and start the process again. Think loving thoughts to yourself and focus on the positive. Give yourself a smile, and continue shopping.

I have often heard these familiar words from eating disorder sufferers: "I hate the way I look. I hate how body image and food obsessions have taken over my life. I am just so disgusted with my body and myself. I hate looking at myself in the mirror. I am just falling apart. I feel like I am totally out of control. I really need some help. I just don't know what to do anymore. I am so, so tired of this. I can't stop crying, and I just never want to eat again."

Acceptance is the key. Accept yourself and your body. How do you get the kind of confidence that creates acceptance? There is no trick to it. It just requires that you work at it, one bite at a time.

Remember: fear of fat equals fear to live life. Let go of the fear, and live your life.

Mirrorless Days

Since mirrors trigger negative thoughts for so many people, limiting contact with them makes sense for many people. It can be a relief to be free of the constant judgment you might be tempted to heap on yourself.

One person in recovery helped create Mirrorless Mondays at her school. It was a day when all the mirrors at her school were covered and everyone spent time focusing on their inner selves instead of their outer appearances. People worked at bringing forth qualities such as kindness, grace, and forgiveness toward themselves and one another. Maybe you could try a mirrorless day for yourself, or with some friends, at home or elsewhere. See if it makes a difference in how you feel.

Recovery Reminders

It can be helpful to have or wear a reminder to stay in recovery mode. Some people choose a special necklace, bracelet, ring, pin, or earring to serve as a reminder to stay positive and healthy each time they see it or touch it during the day. If you decide to try this, choose whatever feels symbolic to you—a butterfly, cross, heart, initial, pretty stone, jewel—anything! If negative thoughts or feelings come up, you can touch your special jewelry and let it remind you of the inner strength you have to heal.

rvlsoft/iStock/Thinkstock

It can be helpful to have or wear a reminder to stay in recovery mode. Choose whatever feels symbolic to you, such as a butterfly, cross, heart, or initial.

Likewise, if you don't want to wear something, you could put something in your pocket, purse, on your desk, in your car, or the like. It could be a rock, a seashell, a charm, a flower, a card, a picture—whatever works for you.

Healthy Thoughts in a Toxic Culture

It is so easy to look around and see messages designed to make you feel bad about your appearance. Often, the messages are specifically designed to increase your dissatisfaction with how you look so that you will want to go on a diet, buy a cosmetic, purchase a magazine or book, watch a TV show, or visit a web page. These messages, and their products, are *not* designed to help you love yourself or your life, even if they say they are. Their main purpose is to make money for someone, somewhere. And many of the images of the people featured in these messages have been digitally altered to impossible human proportions. This constant barrage of false beauty standards can have a toxic effect, and they are hard to escape.

One way to affirm your commitment to health and recovery is to place little reminders throughout your daily environment that encourage positive body image. You can take a stack of index cards or sticky notes and write on them: hearts with kind messages, positive quotes, drawings, nature photographs—anything happy. You might place these healthy reminders right on your mirrors. Some people place them in their car or on their computers. Another effective place might be on the refrigerator or kitchen cupboards. Look for places you see often in your day, and where you might need a little boost of positive messaging.

Weight

While it is true that disordered eating recovery involves far more than a person's weight, it is also true that weight is one marker of health. Often, however, far too much emphasis is placed on a particular number as being an "ideal" weight to strive toward. It will be important for your recovery efforts to create and maintain a new attitude about what you weigh, and what significance you place on that number. It is not easy to change a lifetime of messages you have received and believed about weight, but it is possible and worth the effort, if you want to break free from weight obsessions.

Following are some ideas to help you get started.

Weight Leeway

The medical professional overseeing your physical care will likely suggest a certain weight range for you as you move toward health. Rather than one specific number, a range, such as a 10-pound span, allows you plenty of space to move up and down. This may be adjusted as it becomes more clear where you feel your healthiest, most energetic, rested, focused, and peaceful. No one knows for sure where this will be, but a certain range gives you a goal to start moving toward, even if you end up adjusting it. With the guidance of your medical support person, you should be able to learn where your weight comfort zone will be.

The Weighing-In Moment

The time around a necessary weight check, as you are moving toward health, can feel difficult, for many reasons. Although it may cause anxiety, perhaps you can see it as an opportunity to practice standing up for yourself and what feels right to you. You can't choose whether or not to be weighed as you are regaining your health, but you *can* choose the time of day that suits you best, and even the day of the week you prefer.

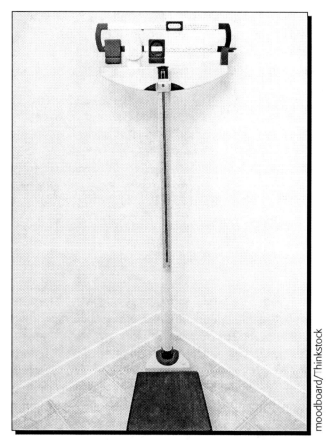

moodboard/Thinkstock

The time around a necessary weight check, as you are moving toward health, can feel difficult, for many reasons. Although it may cause anxiety, perhaps you can see it as an opportunity to practice standing up for yourself and what feels right to you.

Some people choose to be weighed backward and ask that the nurse not say the number aloud, leaving it as helpful information for the healthcare provider, not you. The disordered eating part of your brain will tell you no number on the scale is ever the right number, or good enough. Trust yourself and your healing team to monitor your weight if knowing the numbers is too stressful for you.

On the other hand, you might practice becoming curious about your weight and health by wondering how many pounds it will take to find the healthy, authentic *you* again. You might start to connect feeling energetic, focused, and more peaceful with a certain weight range. That might be your "set point"—the place nature and *your* unique genes have predetermined is your true "healthy" weight.

It's normal for weight checks to bring a mixture of emotions, so plan on doing something pleasurable and nurturing for yourself afterward. Remember, weight is only one aspect of a person in recovery.

The Bully in Your Head

If you have an eating disorder, or suffer from any type of disordered eating, it is likely that negative thoughts about yourself circulate through your brain nearly all the time. If you were to stop and really notice what that voice is saying, perhaps write it down or say it out loud, there is a good chance you'd be shocked by how mean, pushy, and critical that voice is. You could try an experiment where, for one whole day, you actively notice those harsh thoughts and judgments. If you are like most people, you may feel shocked and dismayed by the aggressive tone of that voice. Many have said it sounds like a bully.

Becoming aware of this bully in your head is the first step to defeating it. Following are some tips to help you quiet this voice and create kinder, more nurturing thoughts to guide your recovery efforts.

Eating Disorder Voice

If you're like most people with disordered eating, you know what the bully in your head sounds like and how it wants to limit your life. It tells you things such as:
- Don't eat most food *or* eat so much food that your body hurts.
- Food is bad for your body.
- You're fat, and fat is disgusting. You are disgusting.
- There is nothing beautiful or worthwhile about you.
- You have no friends; no one likes you.

Talk about this inner bully and the negative thoughts it wants you to believe with your therapist. When it gets particularly loud or constant, try writing down what the eating disorder voice says, and then argue with it, in writing or out loud looking in the mirror. This will help you to separate from it and reconnect with the healthier part of your brain that is working so hard. It is time to listen to your positive, healing, nurturing voice. Let your loving voice be the loudest and strongest!

One Bad Bite

The disordered eating bully might try to make you believe that if you take a bite of something that it considers bad, you may as well binge and purge or starve for days because of it. This is all-or-nothing thinking, and something to discuss with your therapist and your dietician. They can help you understand the futility of this kind of thinking and the true science behind eating and how the body makes use of food. Let them help you relearn the truth about eating so you can use that information to silence the bully in your head.

Body Movement

One cold sparkly winter day (actually it was the winter solstice), during my beloved daily walk, with a full moon before me, I remembered when I thought exercise was only good if I hurt afterward. That was when an eating disorder ruled my thoughts and actions. I used to let my boarding school roommates go to sleep, and then I would crawl out of bed and begin an exercise regimen that was more like an act of torture, on a cold linoleum floor. One bite at a time, as I recovered, I learned to embrace the true meaning and feeling of healthy body movement. You don't need to hurt yourself to experience real benefits and pleasure from an exercise routine that heals, not hurts.

Shoulder Rolls

Sometimes, it can be helpful to use gentle movements to calm or soothe yourself when you feel anxious or stressed. Many people carry tension and worries in their muscles, and often in their shoulders in particular. Simply moving them around while incorporating deep breathing can be very helpful.

- Take three breaths deeply into your belly—in through your nose, out through your mouth.
- Roll your shoulders forward seven times.
- Take three more deep belly breaths.
- Roll your shoulders backward seven times.
- One last time, take three deep belly breaths.
- Shrug your shoulders seven times—up—hold for a second, then drop them all at once.
- Enjoy the more relaxed feeling in your body and mind.

This is a helpful routine to use during a stressful time that might have, in the past, caused you to turn to something destructive, such as starving, bingeing, or purging.

Move It!

Somehow, every day, make time for exercise, after getting your doctor's permission. If you are out of balance in this area of your life, you might consider consulting with a fitness trainer or wellness coach who can truly guide you to exercise balance. Each person has to experiment with many kinds of movement to find the best individual exercise routine for her that will bring peace of mind, body, and spirit. The benefits of exercise are far reaching—good for mind, body, and spirit. It is worth getting this area of your life into proper balance so that you can experience the healing energy it can bring.

The benefits of exercise are far reaching—
good for mind, body, and spirit.

Self-Hug

During times of stress, sadness, or loneliness, the body may respond positively to the human touch. It doesn't care if it is you or someone else offering a hug, a massage, or a soft caress; it just wants to be touched with love and care.

Following is how to offer yourself a hug: wrap your arms around yourself tightly, and say or think a loving thought, such as: "It's okay," or "I love you," or "You can do this." Do this often, and you can actually start to feel and believe you're worthy of this loving, nurturing, accepting action.

Creativity and Play

Disordered eating, and all the rules, obsessions, and ruminations that come with it, can temporarily kill a person's inherent creative spark and sense of playfulness. Spending time in creative pursuits and play helps keep your mind healthy, your spirit alive, and your body engaged—all things that will help you turn away from the mind-numbing rigidity of an eating disorder.

Challenge your fears about having to be *perfect* at everything. Try: painting, hiking, fly-fishing, writing poetry, creating collages, or the like. Explore possible life passions without having to be good at them. Just experience the fun of joyful play!

It is such a fun moment in my speaking engagements when people in the audience raise their hands to ask: "Why do you carry a paintbrush during your talks?" I tell them I carry a beautiful paintbrush because it reminds me of one of the most profound life-saving moments of discovery in my recovery.

I found the art room at the boarding school I attended. Immediately my mind and body felt the freedom and non-judgmental acceptance that filled the room. Nothing had to be perfect in there! Whatever I did with paint on canvas or clay was perfect as it was, in its rawest form of expression. Even the girls that were nasty in other settings were nice in the art room. Imagine how my broken spirit engulfed by anorexia and bulimia day and night cherished these feelings. I began to want to be in the art room and feed my soul that energy instead of spending enormous amounts of time calculating and orchestrating a starve, binge, and purge episode.

My answer to the question of why I carry the paintbrush is this: "This paintbrush is dancing in my fingers while I share my journey with you in hopes of encouraging you. It is like my Harry Potter magic wand. May each of you find your own unique paintbrush on the road to recovery."

Scarf Play

Sometimes, an object to which we assign special or symbolic meaning can help us deal with our emotions and/or difficult situations. Some people use jewelry, rocks, charms, or other things. You could also choose to use a scarf, a lovely accessory that can remind you of how to deal with emotions and situations in healthy ways. What follows is one idea for how to do it.

Find three different scarves that serve three different needs: calming scarf, gratitude scarf, and bold scarf. Choose the scarf that best matches your emotions and situations for the day and time. Wrap the scarf—however you want—around your neck and/or heart. You can contemplate your emotions or even express them aloud. As usual, take any raw or deeply troubling emotional needs to your therapist, who will guide your understanding and healing of them.

Eye-Catchers

Defeat negative thoughts by placing eye-catching positivity reminders in your path. Take or find photos of family, friends, beautiful scenery, inspiring quotes, and the like, and place them around your home, office, and even in your car. Negativity can creep into your mind at any time, anywhere. This strategy can help you reroute your thoughts as your eyes catch the kind, loving visuals you've placed in your path. Your mind will stop any hurtful thinking and instead, embrace a happier, more loving thought. Thoughts create emotions, emotions create actions, and actions can help or hurt, depending on which you choose. Change your thoughts, and you change the whole cycle.

Alias-Ching/iStock/Thinkstock

Defeat negative thoughts by placing eye-catching positivity reminders, such as inspiring quotes, around your home, office, and even in your car.

Spirituality

As you read on in this book, you will find an entire chapter on spirituality. It is an important aspect of the healing process and one that requires serious thought and contemplation. You can skip ahead to that chapter now, if you like, or you can read on for some introductory ideas to help you see how spirituality, in any form, can support your recovery efforts.

Please and Thank You

Take your food and emotional fears to a higher power or meaningful spiritual source. Some refer to the higher power they connect with as God, some simply sense a divine order to the universe, which they don't address by name, but do have ways of connecting with. Whatever it is for you, you can try asking for help and emotional healing as you engage in your recovery efforts. You might also be moved to give thanks as you feel healing guidance. Gratitude is a very powerful emotion that can help us focus on the positive and what is working in our lives. Focusing on what we are thankful for can be very soothing.

The quest to find and put faith in something bigger than yourself to rebuild trust and hope is the spiritual journey. This is a journey that can lift you out of the small, narrow path of disordered eating. Each person must identify and develop her own, personal spiritual practices.

I personally wake up before anyone else to grasp the meaning of this every day. It gives me a fresh chance to begin with positive hope and strength. It helps me face the day and whatever may come my way with a strength that does not come naturally to me. This has been a huge part of my own healing progress and triumph as I dug my way out of anorexia and bulimia. Even though I have not starved, binged, or purged for over 30 years, I nurture my spirituality every day. I recommend you explore this powerful healing resource.

Therapy and/or Mentoring

It is very possible that if you are extremely motivated, you can make a lot of progress on your own to change your disordered eating patterns. However, it is strongly recommended that people seeking to fully recover from an eating disorder or disordered eating work with a team of healthcare professionals, which may include: medical care provider, mental health professional, nutritionist/dietician, exercise professional, and a mentor, among others. Medical, nutritional, and exercise professionals will monitor your physical progress and help you construct eating and exercise plans that are safe and make sense for your individual needs.

A therapist or other mental health professional can help you dig deeper to explore any emotional factors underlying your disordered eating. She will help you gain the insight necessary to make lasting changes toward better health.

A mentor is someone who has overcome disordered eating and who can share with you ideas, tools, and strategies to help you find success in your daily encounters with food, exercise, and body image. Mentors are not models of perfection. They are real people, living real lives. They have found their way back to health, and want to help others do the same.

If you can work with both a therapist and a mentor who coordinate their efforts—along with the rest of your team—you will have a powerful support network as you do the hard work of recovery and healing. If there are no mentors in your area, you might look online for digital support. Check out the resource chapter in this book for some ideas.

In this section, you will find ideas and suggestions to help your work with your therapist and, hopefully, your mentor progress steadily toward full recovery.

Roots

What are you really hungry for that has nothing to do with food? Eating for non-hunger-related reasons, or *not* eating when you *are* hungry, can often be driven by intense—and often hidden—emotional pain, which may have roots that run deep in your heart, mind, and soul.

If you experience anxiety, worry, fear, or depression, please seek and develop a positive relationship with a professional therapist so that you can learn to understand these roots and grow beyond them. With this professional help, you will be able to create a path out of your pain and reconnect with your true biological hunger.

Because a counseling relationship requires that you feel safe and trusting, it is important to choose a person with whom you feel comfortable. You may have to talk about difficult things, so the more supported you feel the better. This may mean meeting with several different people to find a good "fit" between you, but it is certainly worth it.

Many people need counseling from time to time to find balance in mind, body, and spirit because life is hard. Become part of a healing team, and accept the help that is there.

Role-Playing

Some people find it helpful to role-play difficult situations that scare them and keep them from healing. You can try this by yourself, or with your therapist, by practicing speaking aloud the words you want to say and the feelings you need to express, which you may have hidden behind your eating disorder. The more you role-play, the better you will get at using your authentic, healthy voice in real-life situations.

I have noticed that there is a personality characteristic in many of us who "choose" the suffering of an eating disorder as our coping skill for life pain. We are really sensitive, "feel-the-seam-in-the-sock" kind of people, so we often are hurt by people's judgments, or perceived judgments. Please work on this tender area with your therapist. She can help you armor up and be more resilient regarding the things people say and do that feel hurtful.

Think about what you are worrying over, or are afraid of, while you are starving, bingeing, perhaps purging, and afterward. Get specific— maybe even write your thoughts down—and take your realizations to your therapist. This is some of the real nitty-gritty work of healing.

I know it is so difficult to stare this stuff in the face! Yet, without this depth of honesty about what really causes your disordered eating thoughts and behaviors, it will be nearly impossible to recover. I speak from experience. I didn't get better until I really dealt with what was wrong. I had to accept the facts: pride, resentment, bitterness, self-pity, sorrow, suffering, loss, grief, humiliation, and my severely alcoholic dad. All of these things played a very important role in sustaining my anorexia and bulimic lifestyle. Recovery began when I accepted the reality that my eating disorder was a life-threatening illness that was covering up the real issues I hadn't yet dealt with. One bite at a time, my healing journey began.

Eat With Your Mentor

When you struggle with disordered eating, you can lose the ability to enjoy socializing and eating at the same time, which can really inhibit your social life. Many celebrations and events involve food, so if food has become a battleground, you can end up sitting on the sidelines, or spending more time alone, which can then exacerbate disordered eating. It's important, then, to start practicing eating with others in a safe environment.

One possibility is to share food with a mentor, if you have one. She represents a positive recovery role model who might inspire you by demonstrating how she feeds herself. If you feel embarrassed to eat at first, start with something simple, like a cup of tea or coffee. As time goes by and your recovery moves along, try having a snack or lunch together—whatever feels most comfortable and least scary. A mentor is probably the least frightening, most trustworthy person you could choose to eat in front of. Eventually, you will become more comfortable eating with others, and can get back into the full swing of your social life.

As a mentor, I find true joy in eating with my clients. It really breaks the fear of social eating so they can enjoy that activity again, and helps them see that someone with an eating disorder really can learn to enjoy eating well again. This hurdle of recovery is huge for people because they are trapped by so many disordered eating fears about what people think about their eating habits.

Write It Down

Because so many important topics may be discussed during a therapy or mentoring session, it is easy to forget some of them afterward. A good idea is to take some index cards and write important ideas, tools, homework, strategies, and such that you want to remember and work on between appointments. Look at the cards each day to stay focused on the work of recovery.

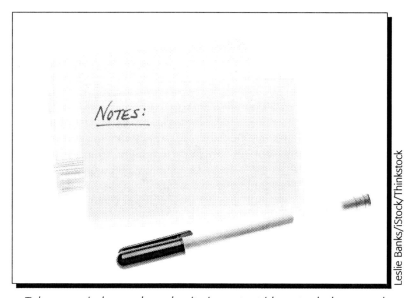

Leslie Banks/iStock/Thinkstock

Take some index cards and write important ideas, tools, homework, strategies, and such that you want to remember and work on between therapy or mentoring appointments.

People and Relationships

There is more to life than food and body image, but when you are struggling to break free from disordered thinking and behaviors related to these things, it is easy to get so wrapped up in recovery work that you neglect the people you love. On the other hand, maybe some of the people in your life contribute to the stress and distress that have led to your struggle. Either way, establishing healthy relationships with the people in your life is a key component to living a full and happy life.

Because relationships can be so complex, you will likely spend time with your therapist discussing important ones and how to improve them. It is hard to give many general strategies that you can apply to all people and all relationships, so as you read the following suggestions, tailor them to fit your life.

Honest and Wise Supporters

Surround yourself with friends who care about you, your healing, and their friendship with you. Reach out, and ask a friend or two to talk openly about how they see an eating disorder destroying your life. Have them name it, and let them say it as nasty as it really is. Let them tell you when they see it surface; listen to how it makes them feel. Your first reaction might be anger toward these friends, but stick with them and say good-bye to any pretend friendship with an eating disorder.

Also, is there someone in your family—past or present—that you respect and admire who seems to be comfortable and healthy in mind, body, and spirit? Can you get to know this person better? Near or far, there is value in connecting with a person within your own gene pool. Obviously, such a person might share how they have developed a wellness program of healthy living. Seek their wisdom and role modeling, and apply some of it to your own life.

Who Do You Really Love?

Who do you love more: family, friends, boyfriend, girlfriend, yourself, life, or your eating disorder? In order to heal, you have to embrace the right love affair, which is with family, friends, and your true self, *not* the lies and empty promises of disordered eating. You can't have both—eating disorders destroy relationships because they demand constant attention and ruin your health. True love and healthy relationships are spacious, emotionally, and build up your health. Which do you really want? Put your healing energy where it belongs!

Make it a goal to spend social time with at least one positive person, at least once a week. People's moods and attitudes are affected by the people they spend the most time with. Consider those in your social network, your family, and your school or workplace. You might even write people's names on a piece of paper or in your journal, and put a star by the ones that seem to bring out the best in you or in others. Plan to spend more time with those people and less time with the ones that seem to be more of a negative influence.

Invite Family to Heal

When one member of a family has a diagnosed eating disorder, or eats in a disordered fashion, the whole family is usually affected somehow. It may even be that another family member is suffering with an undiagnosed eating disorder and the chaos that it creates. Disordered eating does run in families.

If it feels safe and appropriate, you could share your healing journey with any family members that might want to support you, or who seem like they could benefit from seeking their own help. You can't force anyone to seek help, but you can invite them to a therapy session, or to a consult with your mentor and therapist.

Specific Times of Day, Week, Month, and Life

For many people with disordered eating struggles, certain times of the day, week, month, or even year can trigger destructive thoughts and actions. The way to deal with this is head on with a plan of action rather than avoiding the situation or hoping for the best.

Following are some ideas to help you begin to make your own best plan of action.

Nighttime Armor

For some reason, such as not eating enough during the day, boredom, or avoiding unhappy relationships, evening and nighttime often trigger some type of disordered eating experience. By tuning into your body and mind, you can move through that time of day without sabotaging your recovery efforts.

First, tune into your body. Is it giving you clues that you are truly physically hungry? Some people report physical hunger as feeling like an emptiness in the pit of their stomachs, a rumbly feeling and sound, sharp pains, slight nausea, light-headedness, difficulty concentrating, irritability, and so forth. If your body is giving you your particular signals, then feed it! Fix a portioned snack, and eat it mindfully. Do so according to the food plan you are following for your phase of recovery.

If you're not physically hungry, but you're feeling weak about fighting an eating disorder impulse, or you are emotionally upset, depressed, or bored, try one of these ideas: wrap up in a soft blanket, meditate on pleasant thoughts, and fall asleep; then wake up proud you didn't binge and purge. Or, get out your food breaks kit and choose something from it to do. Try getting involved in a creative activity just for the fun of the process, not to create a perfect product. Call a friend. Listen to music.

Make a list of how you can help yourself during your hardest time of day, and turn to it when you need to.

Weekends

Weekends can sometimes bring situations and events, which cause you to sabotage your hard-earned recovery progress. Decide to head into this time period ready to activate all your recovery thoughts, strategies, and behaviors. If you've spent time with your counselor or mentor, that could also help you stay focused.

Plan fun things to do that will recharge you physically, emotionally, and spiritually. Find the balance for yourself between rest time and recreation time. Don't worry about doing things perfectly; your best is good enough.

Seems like, for me, idle time produced way too much time to calculate and execute a starve, binge, and purge weekend. In recovery, the more armor I used, the more distracted from my eating disorder I became, and I ended up feeling good, most of the time. Every success began to add up, and I got better and better.

On the Way Home

It seems so difficult for many people with bulimia or binge eating disorder to grocery shop or run errands and start their journey home without needing to buy some food at a convenience store or fast food restaurant, or get into the grocery bags. Have a plan to deal with this situation. Following are a few great ideas to try.

Have a rebalance kit right beside you in the car. Use it to soothe any difficult food impulses that arise.

Work with your dietician on healthy food choices that you could transfer from a larger bag into a smaller one to enjoy on the way home, and *put the rest of the bag in the trunk*. If you choose to eat in the car—which many people must do from time to time— do so mindfully. Engage in calm, steady, present eating instead of resorting to mindless, absent-minded eating that often happens in cars. You *can* do it; it just takes practice.

You could also find a positive verse or quote to repeat on your journey to help get your thinking in line with your behaviors. Our thoughts affect our emotions and choices; fill your mind with positive thoughts.

Sometimes, returning home to or from stressful situations, like a dysfunctional home life, unrest in marriage, unrealistic expectations from parents, work, friends, or the like, can stir up distressing feelings. If this is the case for you, keep things in your car that will have a calming or soothing effect on you. Perhaps find something to play with in your hand, like a soft, small stuffed animal, a worry stone, or some soft cloth. Use a rebalance kit, listen to music, spritz a nice aroma, and repeat a positive song, verse, or quote. By doing these things, you will reduce the negativity in your mind and body that could lead to a starve, binge, or purge episode.

Tell your counselor if alone time in the car is a disordered eating behavior time because there may be issues like home stress or relationship stress that are behind it. You deserve to be happy as you arrive home.

I used to eat emotionally while driving my car. This often led to stopping to buy foods that I ended up regretting having put in my body. I never even tasted these foods, as ingesting them was a negative stress reaction, rather than a response to physical hunger! So, I used new coping skills and brought kind, calming toys into my car.

I love to squeeze a hacky-sack or gently roll it in my hand. I can process all my emotions by squishing it in various ways. I enjoy smelling a pouch of lavender that a dear friend gave me. I also have a pretty bar of jasmine soap tucked into the car console. I bring greeting cards into my car to look at during red lights or traffic back-ups. They bring joy, memories, and gratitude, which are all pleasant and soothing.

Monthly Cycle

Learn your cyclical feminine flow. As a woman, for many years, if you are healthy enough, you will experience a menstrual cycle. Each month can shake you up a little if you aren't sure where you are at with your feminine rhythms. You would think that you would naturally learn how this affects your mind, body, and spirit wellness. If you do get a little caught off guard, you might begin to get down on yourself. You might feel bloated in special areas like your abdomen, bottom, thighs—and you doubt that what is going on is a natural part of every month since your cycle began.

Don't allow your monthly cycle to become recovery sabotage. Start paying attention so that you get to know what generally happens for your particular body and mind before, during, and after your cycle. This way, you can maintain balance and be kind to yourself during your menstrual process. You might consider putting a little notation on your monthly planner or calendar to help you become aware of what is occurring. Get in the know of your body's rhythm. Be gentle to yourself, understand what is happening, and give yourself permission to flow.

When the Cycle Changes

For various reasons, and at different times, women will stop monthly menstruation. Their cycles may change due to hormones, pregnancy, stress, illness, surgery, or menopause. Eating disorders can also create unpredictability with a woman's cycle.

If you are experiencing unexpected changes in your periods, you should seek medical evaluation. If you are experiencing changes for which you know the cause, it can still be a difficult adjustment, and can bring very real physical and emotional effects. For example, after a hysterectomy or due to menopause, the accompanying hormonal changes can bring about strange new experiences: hot flashes, mood swings, change in sex drive, unintended weight gain, energy shifts, and so forth.

While it is important and helpful to discuss these changes with a health care professional, it is also essential to work on accepting that your body *is* changing, and still requires love, care, and nurturing. Our bodies have an innate wisdom, which includes the need to change as we move through shifting circumstances. Too many women begin to distrust and dislike their bodies as aging or other circumstances change them. This can lead to, or exacerbate, disordered eating.

As your monthly and life cycles change, continue to offer love, acceptance, and nurturance to yourself. Doing so will help you navigate the changes with more peace, and maybe even a sense of humor. If, instead, you feel depressed and out of sorts emotionally, consider seeking therapy. A good mental health professional can help support you as you cope with your changing body.

Special Occasions

Special events and occasions bring excitement and connections with others into our lives. They can relieve the humdrum of daily living, and fill us with joy. However, they can also bring anxiety and fear over whether you'll be able to stay in recovery mode when you're away from the daily routines and patterns you've established.

Planning and preparation go a long way toward helping you enjoy a special occasion without facing disordered eating sabotage or anxiety. Practicing eating with your mentor can also be very helpful in being able to enjoy eating with others. Following you'll find some good examples to help give you ideas about how to deal with your special events.

Planning and preparation go a long way toward helping you enjoy a special occasion without facing disordered eating sabotage or anxiety.

Bring Car Snacks

Travel food and disrupted feeding schedules can be anxiety-provoking if you are trying to change disordered eating habits. One way to help yourself is to bring portioned comfort food that is ready to grab and eat on the road. Put the snacks in trusted containers and snack bags that you use every day to help yourself know how much you're eating, and so that you never have to get hungry between meals or stops. Seek your dietician's advice on what might make the best car snacks for your particular nutritional needs.

Restaurant Idea

Many restaurants serve very large portions of food, which can be difficult to deal with if you have experienced disordered eating and are trying to learn to eat mindfully, tuning into your body's signals as to how much food it needs.

A great way to enjoy a fun restaurant experience and still eat mindfully is to order a go box before your meal even arrives. It can take courage to do this if you are the type of person who has worried what other people think of your food and eating behaviors. Remember, this is about you, not them. You can put a portion of your meal in the go box right away, if you want to, and tuck it safely under your chair, so no one has to see, think about, or judge it. If you want more, you can have it, because you are in charge of how much you eat, not the eating disorder, or the restaurant. Enjoy the whole social eating experience because sharing a meal is a lovely idea!

A great way to enjoy a fun restaurant experience and still eat mindfully is to order a go box before your meal even arrives. You can put a portion of your meal in the go box right away, if you want to, and tuck it safely under your chair, so no one has to see, think about, or judge it.

Why are eating disorder sufferers so afraid to go to a restaurant? Because it feels like a total loss of control! I love going to restaurants, but I had to learn to tackle recovery sabotage around this fun event. Even today, I still tweak the cognitive and behavioral skills I have taught myself during my recovery if sabotage presents itself. One of my favorites is to bring my own salad dressing. I have a little container that is non-embarrassing, fits in my purse, and holds just the amount I know I like.

If this silly skill, or any other positive coping tool, helps you to join your family and friends at a restaurant celebration, then please try it and make it work for you.

Practice, practice, practice, but don't deprive yourself of the fun of eating out with people you enjoy.

Celebrations

This is one of the most complicated territories in eating disorder recovery. Hopefully, you are sick and tired of having the joy drained from a celebration because your eating disorder tells you the birthday cake put before you by people who love you will make you fat.

Try to set yourself up for success. Where can you enjoy a celebratory piece of cake, or other food? Tune in to yourself to figure out what you can handle at any given point of recovery, and then let people know. You might be ready to try eating more freely—a whole piece of cake or just a few bites. If you find it is still too hard to eat a celebratory treat with others, maybe you would like to take a piece home to enjoy at a more peaceful time. Of course, you always have the option to simply say "No thank you."

You need to be your own advocate, letting your loved ones know how important it is for you to feel good in your mind and body. You have to do whatever it takes to feel this feeling instead of constantly trying to please everybody else and hurting yourself in the process. This is tough stuff, and it is how you will heal your disordered eating.

Please care more about the love around you on celebration days than the calories in the food.

Bring a Dish to Share

Along your healing journey, you will be invited to eat with others, which could be an opportunity to bring joy back into your social calendar. Don't turn down an opportunity to eat with loved ones because the negative talk in your head tells you that their food is going to make you fat. You don't want to miss out on social eating experiences and become isolated in a disordered eating world. Instead, accept the invitations and offer to bring something to contribute.

Design a food dish that is created by *you* that *you* will eat. This way, a safe, satisfying food that you trust will be present so that you can eat and share with others. If you want to choose from the food offerings that others bring to the gathering, you certainly can, but either way, you'll know you can meet your nutritional needs while also meeting your social needs.

Sit Healthy

Surround yourself at any and all eating tables with the healthiest eaters you can find. There is no sense in sitting beside people who are using fat language or judging people's plates, including yours. Sit beside people who enjoy food as their fuel and compliments as their chosen conversations.

Find Your Voice

Disordered eating can grow from the behavioral trait of not speaking the truth of how you really feel about many things. You may have developed this habit as a way to survive in a setting where it wasn't safe to speak your mind, or where people told you to keep your thoughts and opinions to yourself. Think about it: starving leaves you too weak to speak while bingeing and/or purging leaves you too busy to speak.

Recovery demands that you find your voice and use it to argue against disordered eating thoughts and behaviors, along with speaking out about the truth of who you are and what you want in your life. Isn't that why you want to recover? To create a life that you are excited about and want to be alive for? Of course! This requires that you muster up your courage and speak your truth.

Grow in Courage

Sometimes, it can help to practice allowing yourself to feel what you truly feel, and say what you need to say. Use props if you need to. You can try wrapping a scarf around your neck and practice being a strong-willed you, and speaking your truth aloud. Find a quiet place where you can be alone and give it a try. What a release this could become for all the emotions that you hold inside and which may have caused you to starve, binge, and/or purge. At first your voice may be soft, but continue to practice, and it will grow stronger and louder.

"I'm *Not* Missing Out!"

This can be your absolute shout-out-loud sentence! If the disordered eating thoughts in your head get too loud and persuasive, talk back to them. Listening to an eating disorder voice can mean missing out on everything in life that is meant to bring you joy. You will be robbed of the desire to be kind to yourself and others. Don't miss out on the good things anymore, and state your intentions out loud—it really can help.

Honesty

Talk honestly about where you are in your recovery process. Are you willing to try? Where are you willing to begin? Write it in your journal, and then share it with your therapist, mentor, or other trusted support person. Be consistent in being honest and journaling, like you were with sticking to your eating disorder rituals.

In recovery, I learned that I eat my feelings. This was a major root of my deadly bout with anorexia and bulimia. It wasn't until I started journaling that I began to see the destructive eating pattern around my inability to cope appropriately with life's stress. That is why I give kudos to emotional journaling along with the wisdom and counsel of your healing team. Remember, you are the one who has to write down your honest feelings. Get them out once and for all.

Privacy

Your recovery is nobody else's business, unless you want it to be. Please don't feel obligated to tell anyone (besides your healing treatment team or trusted, unconditionally loving family and friends) anything that would make you feel less than positive about whom you are and your healing progress. Yes, it's important to be honest and speak up for yourself, but honor your emotional boundaries and only share when it feels safe.

Perfectionism

Oftentimes, underlying disordered eating is the belief that looking "perfect" according to cultural standards will lead to feeling happy, confident, and carefree. Along with that irrational belief might be the hope that if you could do *everything* in your life perfectly, you would feel calm, cool, and collected, and all your problems would be solved.

People who believe that perfection is attainable are often anxious, unhappy, stressed, and lonely, because they are in pursuit of a goal that can *never* be achieved—unless they come to realize that messiness and imperfection is part of what it means to be perfectly human.

If you are a perfectionist, recovery from disordered eating will require that you free yourself from the grip of perfectionism. It can take time and effort, but the rewards will be worth it: more freedom, inner peace, acceptance of self and others, kindness, compassion, and enjoyment of your life. Following are some ideas to help you get started.

I have tried the perfection thing, and it nearly ended me. Finally, I realized that life does not have to be perfect; actually, it cannot be, but it can be just plain wonderful. What a concept! Now I believe it and own that belief. I have found that being grateful allows me to have more good in every day.

Self-Talk

The inner dialogue you have with yourself throughout your day has a powerful effect on your emotions and actions. Perfectionists often start the day with thoughts like these: "I am going to be good today. I'm not going to eat any bad foods, and I will work out harder than ever." Because the list of "bad" foods tends to increase as disordered eating and thinking grow stronger, this can severely limit your food choices, often resulting in starvation, which can then lead to eating mindlessly, which can then lead to thoughts like these: "I wanted to be so, so perfect with everything, and now I went and ate some M&Ms. The whole day is ruined! What is wrong with me? I'm so gross; I'm such a pig!"

This type of downward spiral can lead to more destructive behaviors and thoughts, and it all began with unrealistic and unhealthy expectations of perfection. Drop the expectation, and you'll be surprised at how your attitude toward yourself might shift. You might be able to be more loving and helpful and make choices that nourish your body and mind rather than hurt them.

Embrace "Good Enough"

Perfection: there is no such thing. No matter what other people, magazines, websites, diet books, plastic surgeons, or anyone else tells you, remember that perfect looks, behavior, and thoughts *do not exist*! Try embracing the concept of good enough. A brain entrapped by disordered eating thoughts wants to focus on the things that don't go perfectly: no meals are eaten well enough, no clothes look good enough, no progress is fast enough. Good enough is good enough. Stay on the recovery path, work hard, acknowledge your growth, and live your life.

Rebel!

The right thing to do is not always the right thing that you were *taught* to do. This can be a hard concept for you and/or your loved ones to accept, but it is true. Many people believe the lies about appearance, self-worth, eating, and diets. If you were raised by parents who themselves have (or had) unhealthy relationships with their bodies and/or food, they may have passed on those beliefs and behaviors to you. Not necessarily because they were trying to hurt you, but because it was all they knew. This is true also of friends, coaches, teachers, and others. In order to please those important people in your life, you may have tried to perfectly conform to the standards they set for you, even though those standards were not healthy ones.

As your understanding of health and wellness grows, it may be necessary to reject many ideas you have accepted as true. You don't have to reject the people who taught them to you, thinking they were doing the right thing, but you will have to rebel against all unhealthy and unrealistic ideas regarding weight, appearance, food, diet, and exercise. It can be scary to do so, but it can also be empowering and freeing. Seek support from helping professionals and others who have done the same thing, and you'll be successful.

Setbacks

Because you are a human, and humans make mistakes (from which they often learn the most), you will likely experience a setback or two as you journey toward health. That is normal, acceptable, and just fine. The important thing is not the setback, but that you pick yourself up and get back on track. Right away. What happened happened. Now, in this moment and the next, you can choose to do the right thing, the loving thing, the healing thing. Take a deep breath, and do it. Following are some ideas to help.

Try Again

Whenever you make a mistake or something doesn't turn out as planned, call it a setback, not a failure! Simply try again. Remember, life is full of setbacks. Expect them, accept them, learn from them, and move on.

Why is it so hard to let go of something that is actually hurting you, but has become a way of life? It makes me think of some old shoes I had. They hurt my feet terribly, but I kept putting them on and somehow enduring the pain that shot through my whole body! What I really wanted was a new comfortable pair. So why did I keep wearing them? Habit. False beliefs that I needed to wear them to look acceptable. Laziness. Does this sound at all like your eating disorder? I needed to invest in some new shoes. If you can relate this to your disordered eating, I hope you'll invest in a more comfortable lifestyle and stop hurting yourself.

Behavioral New Beginning

After a bulimic episode or other eating disorder setback, you might feel depleted and discouraged. This is where the meaning of never give up becomes personal. Try these behaviors immediately after a setback.

Take some time to rest, maybe even sleep. Often when you wake up, you will be ready to engage in forward recovery motion. Get your rebalance kit, and freshen up. Call your mentor or therapist for support. If it feels necessary, you could call your healthcare provider also. Follow your dietitian's nutritional recommendations. Nothing is lost. Do the next right thing to keep you in recovery.

After an eating disorder setback, you might feel depleted and discouraged. Take some time to rest, maybe even sleep. Often when you wake up, you will be ready to engage in forward recovery motion.

AnikaSalsera/iStock/Thinkstock

Turn It Around

Face the eating disorder head on. Take your entire mind, body, and spirit and turn 180 degrees away from disordered eating. Take one breath, one bite, and one step forward in the direction of healing. Don't spend any more time thinking about how many times you have starved, binged, or purged your life away until this point. Only *you* can choose to go forward and focus on healing. Turn away from the disordered eating urges to sneak, hide, and lie about food, eating, exercise, and your body.

Triggers

A trigger can be a food that for some reason makes it hard for you to be mindful as you eat it. It may activate urges to restrict or binge. Emotional upsets can also trigger the desire to use food or disordered eating behaviors to somehow deal with the difficult feelings, or to numb them.

It is not a matter of *if* you are going to be triggered during recovery; it is a matter of *when*. Food and emotions are things you have to face and deal with every single day. Staying in recovery is a matter of how you *react* when triggered, not whether you are triggered. Also, triggers actually play an important role in your recovery because they provide a chance for you to practice healthy coping skills.

I had to learn that stress was the root of my eating disorder. I think it plays a big role in others' disordered eating, too. I now accept that I can only do my best to cope with stress; I can't entirely eliminate it from my life. When stress arises, I think (or sometimes even say out loud) thoughts that encourage healthy coping instead of my disordered eating. I might say: "It's okay," or "This too will pass," or "I can handle this," or "Okay, fine." I might even combine a thought with a few deep breaths and some gentle shoulder rolls. If the stress still feels overwhelming, I will ask for help and support from friends, family, or my team of professionals.

Perseverance

Disordered eating didn't happen overnight, and neither will recovery. It takes time, patience, hard work, and perseverance to regain your health. At times, you might feel discouraged or impatient with your level of progress. It is in those times you really need to take care of yourself and ask for help. Following are some words and ideas for encouragement.

Never Lose Hope

Try and try again. Fighting an eating disorder is so hard and often filled with some setbacks. Dig deep for the emotional courage inside of you. Recognize and hold on to the positive moments and every success—no matter how big or small. Patience, persistence, and determination will get you through, one bite at a time.

Practice Persistence

Practice your healing and recovery tools every day for continued health and renewal. You will begin to feel the gift of balance in mind, body, and spirit with newly gained hope, courage, and strength. Own it for *you* this time, not for anyone else.

You can sneak, hide, and lie all the way through treatment, but who wins? Not you! Honestly, I only really started to heal when I realized I was the only one who could heal myself, one bite at a time. I could get support, ideas, and encouragement from others, but I had to do things differently, or nothing would change. No more dishonesty if you want to recover. The question is: do you?

Recovery

The concept of recovery in the disordered eating world is somewhat muddled. Researchers, therapists, clients, doctors, and nutritionists all have different definitions of what it means to be recovered or in recovery from disordered eating. Even the words—in recovery (as used in addictions treatment) or recovered—are not uniform in the treatment world.

Some consider a person recovered when they've reached a healthy weight, have more emotional stability, less compulsive thoughts, and do not engage in harmful behaviors around food or exercise. Some would add to this that a person in recovery accepts her body, is not triggered by food, and eats freely as her appetite dictates. Because there is no clear definition of recovery, each person, along with her team of professionals, must define it for herself, once she is out of serious physical and emotional danger.

You are encouraged to begin to envision for yourself the kind of life you would like to lead once you are not in the grips of disordered eating, and use whatever words you like to describe that. Like life, recovery is a journey and a process, not a destination, so if you are striving to achieve physical, emotional, and spiritual well-being while also leaving behind disordered eating, you are somewhere on the recovery path.

For me, recovery began when I realized I might die if I didn't stop starving, bingeing, and purging my days and nights away. Recovery meant holding an apple and being willing to take one bite, allowing its nutrition to circulate throughout my body, nourish me, and provide energy to my hungry, hollow self. That's how I began recovering, one bite at a time. This was the best I could do on my own, with no consistent outside help. It had to be good enough, and it was. I had already destroyed six very special years of my young life, consumed by anorexia and bulimia, before I became proactive in my recovery.

I have been surprised to find that some people judge each other's recovery as good, bad, or not good enough. As a mentor, I like to focus on—and encourage—progress without the need for perfection. My belief is that recovery means you are trying your best to be the healthiest you can be and you are not in physical or emotional danger.

Over the past 32 years, I have experienced the lows and highs of life: anorexia and bulimia; a severely alcoholic father; the brutal strangulation and murder of my sister along with the grief of her three young children and husband; two beautiful successful pregnancies and births of a son and daughter (during which I gained and lost a total of 100 pounds); my father's suicide, my mom's terrible Alzheimer's and finally blessing her to heaven; a substantial back injury taking me out of the sports I loved; adult bullying; and daily life stress.

I am off-the-charts proud to say that I did not turn to anorexia or bulimia to cope with any of those life stressors over all those years! Instead, I activated, over and over, every cognitive and behavioral positive coping tool I created or learned. They worked in the past and still work in the present. I have been able to stay in balance the best I can. If some skill is not working, I revisit it and make a new version that provides positive direction. Recovery is ongoing for me.

Food, exercise, and spirituality are all intertwined for me. I call it a daily balance maintenance plan with lots of freedom at the foundation. I am not perfect, but I am also not anorexic or bulimic. I have worked really hard to find this authentic me. My heartfelt wish is for everyone's best possible recovery. One bite at a time.

Use Your Intelligence

The authentic you that wants to be well and enjoy your life is smarter than the eating disorder thoughts that have developed in your brain. Call upon that positive intelligence to challenge the damaging eating disorder thinking and its lie after lie! Use it in your self-talk, in your journaling, in your therapy, and any other time when the lies need to be struck down.

Be Willing to Change

You have to be willing to begin, one bite at a time, your healing process. *You are the only one that can accept and live out the cure*. You can read books, go to therapy, visit a dietician, meet with a mentor, keep doctor appointments, but if you don't change your thoughts and actions, you will not recover.

Wake Up!

The more conscious you become of your healing journey, the more aware and enlightened you will become of how unconscious your eating disorder has kept you. Stay awake!

Honestly, my eating disorder experience never had anything to do with food and everything to do with my tender heart, low self-esteem, negative body image, and lack of knowledge about positive coping skills to handle life stress. I truly believed skinniness would solve all my problems, so I starved, binged, and purged my self away. Awaken to the truth: eating disorders don't solve problems; they create them.

Stop in the Moment

Enjoy recovering! Acknowledge and embrace the positive emotions awakening within you. Celebrate your successes. Many people are quick to focus on failure, looking for what went wrong in the tiniest way and focusing on that, rather than on what went right. Unless you take on this new way of thinking, you will remain stuck in negativity and disordered eating. Experience the power of positive thinking: focus your thoughts on what is going well for you.

Treat Yourself to Self-Help Literature

You can gain wisdom from reading good self-help recovery books. As you do so, share what you are learning from them with your healing team. You can also ask your team for some suggestions for quality books or websites. The resource section of this book also has some suggestions.

Remember Who Is in Charge

Make recovery about what you *can* have and do versus the eating disorder constantly telling you what you can't have or do. Take charge of your thoughts and actions and align them with your positive values and goals. This will keep you motivated to create a life you want to be alive for.

No More Lying to Yourself

Recovery from disordered eating requires that you give up sneaking, hiding, and lying. You will have to honestly face yourself with an attitude of tough love in order to move forward. You will have to face your fears, as well as the consequences of your disordered eating thoughts and behaviors. Stop hiding from the truth, and enjoy the freedom of honesty.

Give Yourself a Little Gift

We all appreciate rewards and gifts to help reinforce positive behaviors. Don't wait for others to reward you for your recovery work: reward yourself. You could even put a little gift in a box with a bow on it to give yourself on a day when bulimia or anorexia did not hurt you. It could be anything: a candle, a heart rock, a positive word or quote from a magazine, nail polish, lipstick, earrings, or something similar. The point is to honor your progress. Be proud and bypass the need for perfection. Tell yourself: "You did awesome!" Allow yourself to feel proud and loved—by you.

New Life

Create a new life that includes passion and creativity—however you express them. Ideas you might try include: quilting, horses, painting, clay, singing, dancing, writing, photography, community service—you choose. Recovery requires that you give up all the time you spend thinking about and engaging in disordered eating. With more free time and brain space, you can explore new (or old) interests. This is a very important part of creating your new life.

Don't wait for others to reward you for your recovery work: reward yourself. You could even put a little gift in a box with a bow on it to give yourself on a day when bulimia or anorexia did not hurt you.

Bulimic Recovery

If you are in recovery from bulimia, some people still might not trust that you're not throwing up your food, so one idea is to leave the bathroom door open a few inches. The message will be loud and clear that you're not hiding anything from them, and you're not throwing up. Eventually, trust will be regained, and you won't have to leave the door open anymore.

Bulimia Recovery Savings

Bulimia robs people of a lot of money spent on binge food. If you are bulimic, use receipts to honestly calculate the financial cost of binge-and-purge episodes. It can be substantial, and shocking.

In recovery, try putting that same amount of money into a piggy bank, savings account, or envelope. After a while, go ahead and spend what you've saved on something that joyfully nurtures you. Doesn't that sound better than flushing your money down the toilet?

Practice the Skills

Please refrain from setting a recovery deadline. Be content knowing that the healing process is moving along, one bite at a time. Every person is different and recovers at a different pace.

Practice all the cognitive and behavioral skills you've learned. Use them any time you need to freshen your recovery energy. Continue to create new skills and adjust old ones as life continues to serve up all kinds of experiences. By doing so, you will be allowing yourself to grow stronger—one bite at a time—emotionally, physically, and spiritually. Never, ever give up!

Rimrock Treatment Center

Digging deeper
in this tunnel of heart.
It's dark down here,
so where do I start?

The core is below,
so buried in fear.
I'm cold, all alone,
and hopelessly unclear.

Struggling and searching,
why can't I see?
The answer is waiting,
all within me.

Inside this place,
is calm warm oblivion.
I'm just a disgrace
they call one in a million.

Distract me with letters,
numb me from love,
pray for the better,
then drift like a dove.

Keep up the digging
till I reach the center of my soul.
Pour out the poison,
it's taken its final toll.

—Claire Bachofner

anyaberkut/iStock/Thinkstock

I [Carrie] have kept a journal, off and on, for over 40 years, starting with one of those little five-year diaries that came with a tiny lock and key. I have journaled through the awkwardness of junior high, the anxiety and drama of high school, the beginning and end of one marriage, and for the entire duration of another. I've recorded my thoughts while pregnant with my two children, and my hopes and fears while raising them. I've written about career achievements and disappointments, and about dreams—both the sleeping kind and the waking kind. I've recorded my secret shames and disappointments in myself, as well as the celebrations of my accomplishments.

As a high school English teacher, I asked my students to journal so that they could find their writing voices. By that, I meant their unique ways of expressing their own experiences, feelings, and beliefs. Many of them found that writing freely in this manner became a way to discover how they truly felt about things. They explored their feelings about friends, parents, school, the events in their lives, and their hopes for their futures. I saw many students come face-to-face with some difficult truths they had tried to avoid, only to realize it was time to deal with those things, and seek help and support to do so. Students told me that writing in their journals provided a safe place for them to vent, to dream, to explore, and to get to know themselves better. Years later, many students have told me they still journal because it helps them figure things out. I know how they feel.

Journaling keeps me aware of, and attached, to my soul—for better or worse, in good times and bad. I've known plenty of bad times when it comes to eating and body image. I was teased about my weight all through grade school, which just made me eat more, because eating numbed the bad feelings, temporarily. According to my diary, I was 11 when I went on my first diet. I dieted off and on all during high school, eating nearly nothing for a few months during my senior year. Suddenly, my journals turned into lists of food, calories, and my weight rather than expressions of my feelings. At the time, I didn't notice the change in what I wrote about, nor was I alarmed by it. As happens with many young women, unfortunately, counting calories, berating myself for "failing" to lose weight, and body dissatisfaction had become the norm.

Many years later, when my daughter, Claire, developed anorexia, and I found her lists of food and calories, the shock of recognition was confirmed by my old journals. There were the lists of foods and calorie counts, almost exactly like hers. Recognizing this, I felt physically and emotionally sick. Why did it have to be this way?

During Claire's struggle with anorexia, I journaled like my life depended on it. I was so full of fear, guilt, shame, and anger. My journal became a safe place to contain an experience that so often felt out of control. In it, I told the truth about my daughter, our family, my own disordered eating, and the healing we all experienced through those years. My journal allowed me to see how far we all eventually came, as well as providing a place to express the gratitude and faith it took to get there.

Claire also journaled while struggling with anorexia. It was a huge part of her recovery. A life-long keeper of journals, when she first began starving herself, she stopped writing. She didn't begin again until she was ready to recover. During the healing process, she filled notebooks with her pain, rage, frustration, sadness, and, eventually, her triumphs.

Now that I am a mental health counselor, I have read the research on the positive therapeutic effects of journaling. I often recommend it to clients as a helpful tool for change. Sometimes they bring their journals to our sessions and read from them to help our work advance. For others, the actual journal entries remain private, but the insights they gain from journaling are often key to achieving their goals. I hope you'll consider trying journaling in your recovery efforts.

Throughout this chapter, I'll share more from my personal journaling experiences.

Journaling is a recovery tool you read about previously in this book. It is a powerful resource that can help you in your healing journey and beyond. In this chapter, you will find the following:

- An explanation of what journaling is and how it works
- What you need for journaling
- Some prompts to get you started writing
- Some ideas of what to do with what comes up in your writing
- Some ways to take your creativity and ideas outside of your journal
- Additional ways you can use journaling to help yourself reclaim health and wholeness of mind, body, and spirit

What Is Journaling, and Why Do It?

Journaling is nothing more than writing your thoughts and feelings on paper, in a private notebook or journal. Some people write only about events, some write only about feelings, and some write about both. Some people write poetry or make up stories. There is no wrong or right when it comes to journaling.

Why do people journal? There are as many reasons as there are people that journal. Each individual gets something different out of the experience, though there are some aspects of it that seem almost universal. Some people write so they will remember the details of important events in their lives. Others write mainly to sort out their emotions, paying very little attention to the events in their lives. A lot of research exists to support the notion that journaling assists people who are struggling with some type of emotional or physical stress and/or illness. The mind/body connection is real when it comes to healing. By slowing down and checking in with yourself through writing, you will be connecting intellectually and emotionally to the deepest part of your authentic self. Journaling invites your heart, mind, and soul to join your physical body in the healing process of recovery.

Getting Started

It's very important to understand that your journal is *your* journal. What you write in it is for your eyes only. You may write something that you want to share with someone at some time, but that is not the main purpose. The main goal is to write honestly about anything you want without fear of judgment or criticism.

If you live in a home where you are not sure people will respect the privacy of your journal, then you need to specifically ask for it, or keep it a complete secret that you have one. That may sound contradictory, but it's not really. If you can explain to the people you live with that you are keeping a journal to aid you in overcoming your eating disorder, and that you need to know for sure that they will leave it alone, and they agree to do so, then you won't have to worry about them snooping. It will actually help build trust. On the other hand, if you know that some people you live with aren't trustworthy, you will need to write in your journal in secret and hide it when you are away, or take it with you. It is my belief that you have the right to your own writing space, and no one has the authority to invade that space. Do what you must to guarantee yourself that privacy. Stand up for yourself. If, however, people in your household tell you they will read your journal if they come across it, you may want to bring this issue to the professionals you are working with, and seek their support and advocacy. Trust is a huge issue, and if there is such a lack of trust that you can't journal in private, this is definitely something to discuss in more depth with your therapist.

What will you do with your journal after you've written in it? That topic will be discussed later in this chapter, so keep reading!

Materials

One thing that is very important is to find the right journal for you. It should be one that is, above all else, comfortable and inviting for you to write in.

I like a small notebook with a good sturdy front and back so that I can take it with me outside and not have to hunt for something solid to set it on; I can just hold it in my hands or lap and write. There are many beautiful journals out there with gorgeous covers and fancy paper, and I've owned a few. I filled them up, but sometimes they were more fussy than practical. I've also known people who could not write in a journal because it felt too pretty to them. They didn't want to mess it up by writing about their chaotic lives in it. Other people I know only write in elaborate journals; they are drawn to the beauty, so it helps them write more regularly. There is no right or wrong in choosing a journal, as long as it feels comfortable to you.

Go browse in an office supply store, a bookstore, a gift store—anywhere you think journals and notebooks are sold. Examine closely any that appeal to you. Do you like how it's bound? Does it matter if it's wire bound, or does that bother you? Does it open and lie flat, or would you have to constantly be holding it open or folding it back? Are the lines spaced far enough apart for you to write comfortably? Check out the price—can you afford it? Don't worry if you get one and find out while using it that it's not working for you; you can always get another one. Plain spiral bound notebook, fancy leather covered journal, or artsy covered diary—it doesn't matter which you choose, as long as it feels pleasing to you.

Plain spiral bound notebook, fancy leather covered journal, or artsy covered diary—it doesn't matter which you choose, as long as it feels pleasing to you.

Next, you'll need a good writing utensil. This is *very* important. You've got to find something that, like your journal, invites you to write and makes it a pleasant experience. Journaling is about more than what you say. It's a physical process as much as an intellectual and emotional one. Your hand moves a pen across a page in a notebook. It needs to feel pleasing to you or you won't do it. Finding the right writing utensil for *you* helps make the experience one you'll enjoy.

I like a fine-tipped liquid marker because it feels good in my hand, flows easily across the page, and allows me to write quickly, keeping up with the thoughts that pop into my head. I buy them in a multi-colored pack because I like to switch up colors just for variety. Most people I know that journal regularly don't do so in pencil, because it smears and fades over time. Some type of pen seems to work best, but if you prefer the feel of a pencil, then write in pencil. Whatever works.

I haven't mentioned using a computer for journaling because I believe it's not as effective as writing by hand for allowing you to slow down, reflect, and linger over words and meaning. Certainly, you could try it, and if you like it better, by all means use it. But also try handwriting your thoughts and see if you notice a difference. Then, you can make an informed decision. Privacy on a shared computer is a real issue, too, so take the necessary precautions to keep a digital diary secure.

Writing Routines

When, where, what, and how much you write in your journal will, of course, be up to you. You'll need to experiment to see what works for you. The following sections offer some suggestions for you to try.

For the past several years, I have practiced something called Morning Pages. I first read about it in the book The Artist's Way *by Julia Cameron. She suggests people write three pages every morning, just to clear out the cobwebs of the mind. Three pages may seem like a lot, and it may be too much for you. Some days it is for me. But writing*

early in the morning is a ritual I like. It helps me transition comfortably from slumber to wakefulness. Some days, I don't take the time to do it in the morning because I sleep in or am rushed. If I don't do it in the morning, I will often do it in the evening. I also write when I have a need—if something is bothering me, if I feel depressed, if I am really happy about something, if I have a vague uneasiness, but don't know why. You can open up your journal and write about things whenever you want! I like the ritual of setting aside a specific time to do it, because it keeps me open and in practice with putting my thoughts and feelings into words. Putting things into words and telling the truth is crucial to achieving and maintaining good emotional health.

When to Write

First thing in the morning, when households are usually quiet, and before the rush of your day gets started, you might find that your brain is able to focus in a more relaxed, open manner as you write about your life. Some people find that incorporating a few minutes of journaling into their morning routine helps them start their days feeling more calm and centered.

If you aren't a morning person, or there is simply no extra time, try journaling at the end of the day. Writing can be a great way to process the events and emotions of the day, now that you have time to focus. If you're like many people, your day can fly by so quickly sometimes, that it seems all you can do is react, all day long. Taking time to check in with how you feel about what has happened, and how it relates to stress, anxiety, body image, and eating can really open your eyes as to how these things are connected, and what you can do about it.

Some people take their journal to a coffee shop or library or even to their cars in the middle of the day, finding rest and refuge in this private space. It can become a mid-day break that opens your eyes and awareness so that, if you need to make adjustments in your day, you can do so.

If you are an active dreamer, or struggle with insomnia, keeping a journal by your bed can be helpful. Recording your dreams can provide some interesting ideas to share with your therapist. If you have trouble sleeping, writing about how that feels, what is on your mind, what you wish could happen, or even doing some creative writing can be helpful.

Try writing at several times throughout the day and see if a specific time of day works best for you, knowing, of course, that you can always change your mind. Don't get rigid about it. That will just make you anxious, and you certainly don't need that!

Where to Write

You can write wherever you want to. It seems that, to really be able to stick with it and focus, you should choose a space that allows you to tune out the rest of the world, and tune into yourself. People journal in the following places:

- Bedrooms
- Desks
- Beds
- Coffee shops
- Libraries
- Parks
- Wilderness
- City benches
- Cars
- Buses
- Airports
- Beaches
- Schools
- Waiting rooms
- Tables

Obviously, you can journal almost anywhere. Try several different places.

What to Write

Once you have gathered your materials and found a time and private place to write, how do you get started? First, commit to the following: You will always tell the truth in your journal, no matter how difficult. The truth may be hard to express, at first, but it is crucial if you want to heal. Following are some prompts to get you started.

General Topics

- Write about what you've been doing lately—homework, school, job, family events, things with friends, hobbies, and such. Try to describe the events in detail.
- Now, write how you feel about the things you've been doing—what do you find satisfying? What do you not like? Why?
- Describe some of the people in your life, in detail: looks, personalities, hobbies, ages, relationship to you, and so forth. Also describe how you feel about these people. Be *honest*! Remember, no one will read this but you, and if you don't like having the truth about your feelings lying around after you've written them, you can always remove the pages and destroy them. Your journal may help you recognize and remember important things, but if it makes you uncomfortable to have your

true thoughts out there in black and white, you can destroy the pages, knowing that doing so won't destroy the truth of your feelings.

- Write about important things you remember from different ages in your life. Why are they important to you? What feelings do you associate with these events? You might go back as far as your memory allows, and then work your way up to present. Try one thing for each year of school, and then move onto important experiences of adulthood.
- Write about romantic relationships, attachments, or crushes you have had. What attracted you to these people? How do you feel about them now?

Getting to Know You

- Make a list of your favorite things: music, movies, TV, sports, friends, family, places, classes, animals, trips, clothes, stores, artists, and so forth. Pick one or more of the things you listed, and write more about it: a detailed description and your feelings.
- Make a list of your *least* favorite things, and describe some of them in more detail.
- What are some hopes you have for your future? These can be career, relationships, adventure, wild dreams—anything! Why do you hope these things happen? What are some things you will have to do to make one or more of them a reality? Is there a small step you can take toward one or more of them right now? What scares you about these things? How will you overcome your fear, if you want to?
- Describe yourself as you think your best friend would.
- What are your strongest qualities that have nothing to do with appearance or looks? How can these qualities help you achieve health and your greatest hopes?

Family

People don't get to pick their families, but they are all part of one, for better or worse.

- Name some of the "better things" about being a part of your family; then name some of the "worse things."
- What can you learn from being a part of your family that will make you a stronger person?
- Who in your family do you feel closest to? Why?
- Who in your family would you like to feel closer to? Why?
- Who in your family do you worry about? Why?
- How has your disordered eating affected your family? How do you feel about that?
- Describe the role of food in your family. Is it used in celebrations? Is it something not much thought is given to? Or can you recognize some food obsessions in your family members?
- Are others in your family struggling with food or body image issues? How do you feel about that?

- Who in your family is the most supportive of your recovery? Why? If no one in your family is supportive, to whom outside of your family can you turn?
- Some families experience trauma (very upsetting events), or some members of the family do. Things like: death, divorce, addiction issues, abuse, job loss, and the like. If any of these issues have been in your family, or have happened to you, try writing about them, including your feelings. Many times these types of issues are involved in disordered eating. Understanding struggles with your family traumas can help you achieve better emotional and physical health.

Disordered Eating and Body Image Topics

- Remember back to when your disordered eating habits began. Describe what was going on in your life and how you felt about it. Who knew about what you were doing? What was their reaction?
- Talk about your disordered eating habits and rituals today. Be specific and detailed. How have they changed since you first began? How do you feel about them now?
- Describe how you feel about your body. Be honest.
- How do you *feel* about how you feel about your body? Again, be honest.
- List things you like and/or respect about your body, such as, the fact that it keeps oxygen flowing in and out of your cells, 24/7, and you really don't even have to ask it to do so.
- What would you like to change about your body image and disordered eating so that you could enjoy life, people, and yourself more? What are you doing to make these changes happen?
- What are some of your fears? These can be about anything, real or imagined. Talk about exactly what it is you fear about these things.
- Write a letter to your eating disorder voice. Give it a name. Many people name that voice ED (for eating disorder). Tell ED your real feelings about the things it says to you. Be honest and blunt. Tell ED your hopes and plans regarding recovery and health, and be bold about it.

Your Worldview

- Describe your moral code of ethics. What things do you believe are right, and what things are wrong? Why do you believe this? What and/or who influenced the development of your sense of right and wrong?
- How well do you live by your own code of ethics? When have you fallen short? When have you stood firm? How did you feel in those situations?
- Do you believe in God or a Higher Power of some sort? Why? How do you think God or the Higher Power feels about you? What kind of help do you need or want from God or a Higher Power as you recover from disordered eating? Why?

- If you don't believe in God or a Higher Power, what thing bigger than yourself do you connect with: nature, art, music, philosophy, science, the cosmos? How can your belief in this thing (or things) help you to live a healthful, peaceful life?
- What problems or issues in the world today concern you? Write about what you can do to help solve that problem, both in small ways and larger ways, now and in the future.

*What thing bigger than yourself do you connect with:
nature, art, music, philosophy, science, the cosmos?
How can your belief in this thing (or things) help
you to live a healthful, peaceful life?*

Say It Another Way

- Write your autobiography—so far—using a third-person narrator. For example, if a person named Jane were doing this, she'd say: "Jane was the first child born to her parents. She grew up knowing a lot was expected of her. Sometimes she could meet those expectations, and sometimes she couldn't, but she always felt them, and she always tried." Writing like this allows you to look at yourself and life from a new perspective, a different one than you've become accustomed to. Doing this allows you to write the story of your life with you as the main character, moving through conflicts, in different settings, interacting with other characters, and such. A new way of seeing yourself is what recovery is all about, and this writing exercise might help.

- Write a poem. Maybe you'll find some powerful ideas in some of your journal entries that would make a strong poem. Remember, poems don't have to rhyme (they can, but they don't have to); they just have to be honest, use bold, powerful words, and be artfully arranged on the page.

- Write a short piece of fiction. What about? Anything! You can base it on events from your own life, but make things turn out differently than they actually did. You can base it on someone else's life. You can be totally creative and make it about a make-believe world. All you need for a short story are: characters, setting, problems that need to be worked out, and the working out of those problems. Many authors say writing fiction is the best therapy they've ever had because it allows them to explore, through fictional characters, the issues they have encountered in their own lives.

- Write an essay. No, not the kind where you have to cite sources and worry about a grade, but the kind where you pick a topic and simply write what you think about it. Try topics related to what you are interested in or care about. See if you can pinpoint a problem or challenge and describe a solution; this could be in your own life, your family, your town, your country, the world at large. This is what bloggers do every day. Try it. Maybe you'll get so good at it you'll set up your own blog!

- Write a letter to someone saying what you always wanted to say to that person. Don't have the intention of sending it—just do it to experience what it feels like to say the things you need to say. Maybe you'll want to share this with your therapist, maybe you'll want to edit it and send it, or maybe you'll want to rip it to shreds. The choice will be all yours.

Writing Time Length

If you are new to journaling, you might want to start with some short writing periods, say 10 or 15 minutes. You can write longer if you want, but please, don't turn this into another rigid ritual. Just try some different lengths of time.

If you are writing about a very intense experience or emotion, you might want to limit it to no longer than 30 minutes so that you don't get stuck in the experience. Setting a timer can help you put a boundary around what might be a difficult experience. When the timer goes off, finish up, set your pen down, breathe deeply, and then move onto some type of pleasant, calm, nurturing experience. Take the journal, or at least the ideas and feelings that came up, to your therapist.

Once again, please remember: there is no right or wrong on how long to journal. Experiment, play around, be curious, and be open.

So You've Journaled—Now What?

Now that you have filled up several pages, notebooks or journals, what will you do with them? That is totally up to you. Following are some ideas:

- Read back over your journal entries before going to an appointment with your therapist. Jot down anything that seems important to discuss there, or just make a mental note. Some people take their journals with them to these appointments and actually read directly from them to the professional.
- Read back over your journal entries, and see how far you have come. If you have not yet committed to gaining better health, look back over your entries for evidence that maybe it's time to start seeking professional help.
- Tuck your journal away and decide what you want to do with it later.
- Discard your journals, especially if rereading them makes you feel sad and mad at yourself. Simply throw them in the garbage, or create a little ritual by burning or shredding them, and realize how far you have come.
- Look for passages that show your wisdom and strength. Highlight those areas to turn to in times of weakness or doubt. You could even copy those passages down in colorful ink and make them part of a collage or frame them. These nuggets of wisdom are hard won, and there is nothing wrong with honoring your work by honoring your words.

The main thing to remember is that journaling is a tool to help you in your recovery journey. It may be one you find tremendous power in using, or it may not appeal to you. Either way, it's okay. It's your choice and your decision, and you can always change your mind.

In Flux

A skiff of snow yesterday
and the thermostat battle is on.
Sweat beads turn to goose bumps
as we shiver through our days.

Then, suddenly, pumpkin pie.

We are cocooned in low light,
narrow window of activity.
We are dazed in the limbo of dusk and dawn.
Pressure of a blazing blue sky has lifted,
and so we sigh and settle into
our winter selves.

We stow quick searing barbecues,
unearth our trusty slow cookers—
savory fog on windowpanes.
The scent of the next hardy dish sprawls out.
We knit, weaving tangled nests of loose yarn
into thick wooly scarves.
And breathing deeply,
we take our time.
Hour after hour,
we simmer and settle.

Skiers take inventory
find five-dollar bills in last year's pockets,
dripping hot wax from
edge to edge
they create even planes and dream of
stealthy speed
just beyond their reach.

Ice fishermen trade graceful fly rods for
short stumpy sticks,
gas up their augers and
arrange into neat stacks
their trusty blue tarps,
wide eyes glued to the surface of a favorite lake.

Bird songs, now too distant to hear.
The wind sings its lonely tune.
Degrees fall out of the air
like the steady drip of an icicle,
and hot coffee has never tasted so good.

—Claire Bachofner

smazkul/iStock/Thinkstock

What is mindfulness? Perhaps a good place to start in understanding this concept is to look at its opposite: mindlessness. Many people engage in mindless activities, like: Internet surfing, television watching, driving familiar routes, and (of course) eating. For a variety of reasons, minds tend to take breaks from awareness as people go about their activities. It may be that they are bored with their routines, that they feel stressed from thinking or doing too much, or it may be a coping mechanism their brains latched onto when being aware of what was happening was too painful to endure. Whatever the reason, when minds disengage from their experiences frequently, a split may develop inside people with damaging consequences, including, possibly, disordered eating behaviors. If mindlessness is part of the problem, then mindfulness is part of the solution.

Mindfulness is not a new idea. Cultivating conscious awareness of the present moment—along with the thoughts and actions within it—is a practice that has been taught and followed all over the world in many cultures and traditions, first as a spiritual concept, and, more recently, as a research-proven method for gaining greater peace and wellness, apart from any specific spiritual framework. It is a case of ancient wisdom becoming modern medicine, thanks to scientific exploration that has recorded and validated its power. For a detailed understanding of the research and findings, please refer to the resources chapter of this book.

In a nutshell, mindfulness simply means acknowledging that life unfolds one moment at a time, and in each moment we have a choice of what to think, feel, and do. In addition to engaging in mindless behaviors that take people away from present moment awareness, many have developed the habit of either reliving the past or worrying about the future, which prevents them from living in the present as it is happening. In other words, as life is unfolding right now, they are captivated by thoughts of past and future moments so much so that they miss the only moment they truly can experience: this one.

How is this relevant to disordered eating recovery? By striving to fully inhabit each moment of their lives, people can discover those in which their minds seek escape through disordered eating and the thoughts that fuel it: comparison, judgment, criticism, shame, guilt, and so forth. With that discovery also comes the realization that there is space—however small it may at first seem—to make a different choice: a conscious, loving, compassionate choice to care for themselves deeply in those moments. Moving away from the powerful and destructive automatic thoughts, beliefs and actions of disordered eating is what the recovery process is all about. Mindfulness offers a powerful framework for change, especially when combined with specific, concrete options you can turn to once you realize you have a choice.

So how do you put into practice the concept of mindfulness? Of the many ways, a few ideas of how to begin are described in the following pages. The resource list at the end of this book contains more terrific resources where you can learn about, and practice, mindfulness.

Mindful Attention to Thoughts

Many people have little conscious awareness of how their thoughts affect their moods and choices, eating disordered or not. A branch of psychology called cognitive behavioral therapy says that if people can learn to become aware of their thoughts, they can change them, and if they change them, they will feel better emotionally and, thus, behave in more satisfying ways.

Sadly, many people who develop eating disorders have been bombarded with negative, critical, and shaming thoughts about food and their bodies. In Chapter 5, you can read about "the bully within," a metaphor for the harsh inner critic that circulates negative thoughts in an eating disordered brain.

Many people wonder where that voice came from and what they can do to stop it. Some people can identify sources of the voice: parents, teachers, bullies, friends, enemies, lovers, magazines, websites, siblings, coaches, babysitters, bosses, coworkers, and on and on. Others can't specifically identify who may have talked to them in such harsh terms. Either way, at some point in their lives, people with eating disorders came to believe the things they heard from people and/or the culture at large, and those messages developed into a thought loop, or voice, that plays loudly and constantly in the background of everything they do. And slowly, over time, it crushes their spirits, narrows their worlds, and harms their bodies. The first step to turning down the volume of that voice is to notice it. Once you've noticed it, you can begin talking back to it in powerful ways, challenging the lies it tries to get you to believe. It is hard work at first, but gets easier with practice.

Another habitual thought loop that can develop in people with disordered eating is constant comparison and judgment of themselves and others. This can take the form of walking into a room and instantly sizing up everyone in order to: feel good if they judge themselves as the smallest person there, or feel bad if they believe someone else is smaller. Either way, the judgment is used to fuel the compulsion to starve, binge, purge, overexercise, and such. It is a never-ending cycle of dissatisfaction that ends in exhaustion, isolation, and despair. How do you break free from this cycle? Read on for some suggestions.

Changing habitual thoughts requires patience, humility, self-compassion, and support. A helpful approach is to notice destructive thinking as it is happening, stop, breathe (deep breathing calms your nervous system), and acknowledge that you are engaging in negative thinking patterns. Then, take another deep breath and think loving, positive, kind things toward yourself such as: "It's okay. I don't have to stay stuck in these thoughts. I am good and lovable just as I am. No need to compare or judge. I am on my own path to health. Others are on their paths. Be in this moment."

A metaphor I [Carrie] offer people I work with is to think of the harsh, critical voice as coming from a radio with a volume button on it, and the loving, compassionate, healthy voice they are developing as also having one. I suggest they visualize turning down the loudness of the critical voice while turning up the sound of the loving, healthy voice.

Becoming aware of your thoughts and noticing when you are listening to bullying or destructive thought loops allows you to exercise the power to choose what to do next: continue to pay attention to, and be ruled by, the critic or pay attention to, and be supported by, the loving voice of good health.

Mind and Body Connection

Research has proven that learning to quiet the mind and body helps relieve depression, anxiety, stress, and perfectionist tendencies—all of which accompany disordered eating. If you can learn to quiet your mind, you can also become more attuned to your true emotions and needs, so that you can make healthy choices to fulfill your actual needs, not your habitual ones.

Some formal practices that help people become more calm and centered include: meditation, yoga, prayer, writing, gentle walking, focused deep breathing, guided

Some formal practices that help people become more calm and centered include: meditation, yoga, prayer, writing, gentle walking, focused deep breathing, guided relaxation soundtracks, and stress reduction courses based on mindfulness concepts.

relaxation soundtracks, and stress reduction courses based on mindfulness concepts. One practice—deep breathing—is described in the following section, and you can find more resources at the end of the book.

Focused Deep Breathing

People's manner and rate of breathing sends signals to their brains about their state of calm or anxiety. Rapid or shallow breathing is interpreted by the brain as danger or stress, which raises the body's anxiety level. Deep, relaxed breathing that inflates the belly tells your brain that everything is fine and it's okay to relax. This is an important skill because, oftentimes, it is imagined stress and anxiety that trigger eating disordered thoughts and behaviors. Having the ability to calm and soothe yourself is critical to recovery.

To learn this type of breathing, follow these steps:
- Sit in a comfortable chair, or lie down.
- Feel your body in the chair, or against the floor. Allow the full weight of your body to rest fully on the chair or floor.
- Slowly inhale deeply into your belly, like a sleeping baby does, or as if your belly were a balloon you were inflating.
- Hold the breath in for just a second, and then slowly let it out. Don't force it too much one way or the other—just breathe into your belly and out.
- Breathe through your nose, not your mouth.
- You can think thoughts with each breath, if you like, that encourage relaxation, calm, and peace, such as: "I'm okay. Everything is fine. I am healthy and healing. I am at peace." Or, you can think something like: "I breathe in peace; I breathe out fear. I breathe in love; I breathe out judgment."
- Allow the muscles in your chest, back, neck, and shoulders to relax more with each breath.

At first, try to do it for at least a minute, a few times a day. Then, add another minute to this exercise. Work up to about five minutes at least once a day. Once you have learned formal breathing like this, you will be able to use your breath to calm and center yourself all through the day, in many situations, including with food, people, school, work, and other places. It is a free tool that you always have with you, and which has no negative side effects.

Mindful Eating

Because recovery from disordered eating requires you to relearn hunger and fullness cues, the ability to be fully present during mealtimes can be extremely helpful. Eating mindfully means eating with full awareness of the food, the setting, your body's needs, and the emotions present. One way people unlearn their natural cues about hunger and fullness that all people are born with is by doing other things while eating which distract them from their bodies, such as reading, watching TV, driving, texting, talking on the phone, surfing the web, and such. Another way we learn to ignore our inborn cues is when other people interfere with comments like, "You're not going to eat another cookie, are you?" Or, "Is that all you're going to eat? Have more!" Mindful eating requires that you just eat, tuning into your own internal experience, while perhaps gently socializing if you are eating with others.

What does a mindfully eaten meal consist of? Food that has been chosen using the recovery guidelines you are currently following; tableware that is pleasing and fits the food; a nice setting, and maybe some pleasant company, if it is not too distracting.

Next, the way you approach your meal, emotionally and intellectually, makes it mindful or not. If you eat too fast, you don't give your mind and body enough time to make the most of it. Try starting a meal with gratitude and/or appreciation for it and how it has come to be at your table. This food, which has likely come from many varied places, thanks to many people and resources, is going to make it possible for you to live your life. Take a few seconds to become aware of food as your life support, not your enemy.

Notice also the full sensory experience of eating: sight, smell, touch, taste, and sound. Eating is a sensual experience involving every one of our senses. Not many experiences are that complete. See if you can identify the five senses involved in eating your food.

Between bites, take a few seconds and let the food enter your body peacefully. Chew and swallow, notice how you feel, perhaps sip a beverage. If you feel anxious, take some deep breaths. If you feel sad or worried, offer yourself some kind, compassionate thoughts. Then, take your next bite and repeat.

After your meal, take a few moments to send positive, loving thoughts to yourself for nurturing your body, mind, and spirit with food. Then, clean up your dishes and move on to the rest of your life. Some people clean up their food preparation dishes before they eat, so that right after a meal, they can be done with their food experience and move on. See what works best for you.

Mindfulness of the Moment

Life unfolds one moment at a time, and if you want to experience being alive as richly as possible, then you need to try to keep your awareness on each moment as it happens. It's a simple concept that can be very hard to do. This fast-paced world often requires a person's attention to be scattered in order to keep up. Work, relationships, leisure time, and family obligations intersect and overlap, thanks to technological devices that can keep you digitally connected to everything, all the time. However, this kind of connection is not the same as when you connect by being fully present with the person, task, experience, emotion, or thought that is occurring in the moment—right now. Think of digital connections—as wonderful as they may be—as junk food, and face-to-face connections as a mindful meal. Both nourish the relationship, but one is more satisfying and longer lasting.

Another way people are pulled out of the present moment is by ruminating about past experiences or worrying about future ones. Reflecting on the past can help you learn and make sense of your life, but replaying, over and over, things that have happened, especially negative things, can keep you stuck in the past so that you miss your present experiences. Similarly, you have to do some planning for the future so that you have direction in your life, but to focus most of your attention and energy on things that have not happened—*and may never happen*—is, again, to miss out on the only moment you are guaranteed: this one.

Increasing momentary mindfulness is very possible; it just takes practice. Some simple ways to get started include:

- Turn off technology for a certain amount of time each day in order to focus more on real-life experiences.
- If you have children in your life, get down on the floor with them and either play with them on their terms, or simply observe them and notice every little thing they do. If your mind wanders, bring it back gently to the present moment and the little person you are with. Pets offer similar chances to be fully present with a playful attitude.
- Be fully with other people—one at a time or in groups. Listen as they talk without thinking of what you want to say. Look at their face, their body. Give them your full attention—a rare gift nowadays.
- Take a sensory walk outdoors. For a minute or so, notice sights, and name them as you see them: tree, flower, bee, cloud, sidewalk. Then switch to sounds, and name them: car, dog, cat, leaves, airplane, wind chimes. Then, go through the other senses: smell, touch, taste. You might surprise yourself at the things you discover that have been there all along. If you can't go out for a walk, just sit or stand near an open window or door, or just turn off the TV, radio, computer, and the like, and see what you hear, smell, and so forth.
- As you are doing a simple task, such as washing dishes or showering, try to notice the smells, sights, and textures as you experience them. Name them, and let yourself fully feel the soap or the bubbles or the water.
- Sit quietly in a chair, or lie down, and become aware of your breathing. Don't change it; just feel the air coming in through your nostrils and down into your lungs, then notice the exhale as the process reverses. Try counting each one, up to 10. If you lose track, start over, without judgment.

Annie Crandall Campbell

*Take a sensory walk outdoors. For a minute or so,
notice sights, and name them as you see them:
tree, flower, bee, cloud, sidewalk.*

Research has shown that not only do these practices help people feel more aware and tuned into their experiences and feelings as they happen, it helps them in their day-to-day tasks also. Successful eating disorder recovery asks that you stay fully aware of your thoughts and emotions so that you can make healthy, honest choices. Mindfulness practices help you develop the awareness, strength, and emotional balance to do just that.

Surfing the Urge

When the urge to restrict, binge, or purge (through vomiting, exercise, or other means) arises, it can be so intense that you feel you must give in or you won't survive. In the world of chemical dependency, people say the strong urge to use a particular substance is like an ocean wave in how it arises in the mind, builds in intensity, and then drops off. If people can learn to surf the urge wave without being sucked into it, they will be more successful in freeing themselves from addictions. The same can be said for the urges related to disordered eating.

Using mindfulness, you can notice when the urge to engage in disordered thinking or behaviors starts, and then turn to a calming or coping strategy to help you through until the urge dissipates. Many coping or calming strategies are available for you to turn to, including those described in this book. What might be most helpful is to create a list that is personally relevant and helpful to you, such as: listen to music, paint your fingernails, brush your teeth, stretch, play with a child, gently walk the dog, light a candle and breathe, and so forth.

The more you practice this skill, the stronger you will get, and the less urgent your urges will feel. *You* will be in control in those moments, rather than those moments being in control of you.

Pause

I wake up with reluctance and offer
"Good Morning"
to my beloved mutt who
wags, stretches and sometimes winks
on our way to the cold
(crumb-littered)
linoleum
where we trip
over
my compulsive overeater cat who bats my ankles
until I sprinkle clanking bits
in his silver dish that I purchased from the thrift store
with something much more lavish in mind.
Once my limbs fall into the sleeves of decent clothing and
I swallow a fistful of vitamins and
play a nice game of hide and seek with my car keys,
I scowl at my reflection one last time
before escaping into the chill of a brittle autumn morning.
On the drive, I try to sing through the CD skips and wonder
if my mother ever owned
anything scratched
except me.
If I park far away it's because I'd rather walk
than compete with all the other cars
plus, parallel parking
makes me sweat.

I lock up as Anxiety approaches and takes my hand.
We breathe and march on,
over crippled sidewalks and dusty streets,
past perfect lawns and frozen gardens
glimpsing the lives of others—we note:
a rusty Radio Flyer here,
a pair of ceramic bunnies there,
cracking plastic Frankensteins and
out-of-season bee traps.
If we're lucky, our routine is obstructed.
Just yesterday, amidst all of this hum-drum bullshit,
the air stirred,
and an urgent wind sifted through the skeletal remains
of a summer maple
then through what remained of me and
I stood,
small and still—a shaken witness
as the leaves drifted down, reluctantly,
all around me,
like refugees,
disconnected in a
cruel new world.

—Claire Bachofner

Many people who have recovered from eating disorders say that connecting with something bigger than themselves and their struggle was, and continues to be, extremely important in staying healthy. This type of connection can be called spirituality, because it is about enlivening each person's inner spirit and connecting to the larger web of life and love all around. For some people, spirituality can be expressed through formal religious devotion; for others, it may be expressed in different ways. Read on to see ways to explore spirituality on your own.

Spending Time in Nature

The natural world holds great potential to heal emotional wounds. The five senses come alive in the presence of mountains, deserts, rivers, oceans, lakes, meadows, forests, and wildlife, pulling people out of the mindlessness to which they may have become accustomed. By experiencing the natural rhythms of life—daily and seasonally—you realize there is an order and power you can count on. You can feel yourself both a part *of* it, and apart *from* it, as the days and nights, sun and moon, continue on their ancient journeys. This kind of awareness can help you realize the futility and pointlessness of trying to maintain an eating disorder. It goes against nature. It takes you out of living in harmony with your body's natural rhythms, and the greater rhythm of life all around you, and of which you are a part.

Annie Crandall Campbell

*The natural world holds great
potential to heal emotional wounds.*

What if you don't live close to nature and can't get into "wilderness" very often? You may have to look harder for it, or even cultivate nature in your own home with plants, rocks, water features, but it is all around you. Look up: there's the sky and the cosmos. Look down: there is the earth; even if you live in the city, can you find places where you can see dirt? Or can you bring plants and living flowers into your home and nurture them? Look around: can you find animals, insects, water, trees anywhere near you? Or perhaps you can plan to take a trip into a natural setting for a day or weekend. Be creative and see where it leads. Nature is all around you and in you; you are a part of the landscape of life.

Social Causes

Many people find the experience of volunteering with organizations and working for causes they believe in to be very beneficial in moving away from disordered eating thoughts and behaviors. You can give your time and attention to many needs, which can help create healing in your community and in you. Find a cause you believe in, and donate some time to it: environmental, preventing child or domestic abuse, hunger/food/water issues, the arts, poverty issues, animals, human rights, and so forth. Most people experience increased mood and well-being after doing something to help others and/or their community. It can make your life feel more meaningful to contribute to the greater good. You can ask around about opportunities, check with schools, churches, food banks, or other organizations, or do an online search for volunteer opportunities near you.

Philosophical Explorations

People have been trying to understand the meaning of life and existence forever. Many people have dedicated their lives to exploring possible answers by engaging in philosophy, the study of meaning, knowledge, wisdom, ethics, and the like. Learning what great thinkers have come to believe about what makes life meaningful can be both intellectually and spiritually engaging. Many who study philosophy find that asking the big questions and exploring possible answers are as rewarding as solving the puzzle. If nothing else, reading and discussing the big ideas that have shaped many cultures can help you understand that you're not alone in seeking meaning for your life. Learning what people have discovered as they have pondered these deeper questions is very interesting, and can be quite inspiring.

How to begin? Some websites to visit are listed in the resources section of this book. Additionally, you could check with a local college or library for classes, books, or discussion groups. Ask around—maybe some friends would enjoy getting together and talking about philosophy. You could start your own philosophy club.

The Arts

You probably know what it is like to be carried away by a favorite song, or to get lost in a book or movie, or become one with a beautiful dance, or to be astounded by a work of visual art. Many would consider these experiences to be spiritual in that they lift us up and away from our ordinary, day-to-day experiences, allowing us to feel more profoundly alive.

Both creating art and enjoying it can be uplifting. If you have a favorite artistic pursuit or appreciation, by all means include it in your recovery efforts. Some people find they can express the powerful emotions they experience during eating disorder recovery through artistic means.

If you haven't experimented with creating or exploring art, you could look around in your community for classes, events, shops, and organizations. You could do an online search to find art events near you. The resources section of this book lists some websites that help you explore your artistic self.

You can't "do" art wrong, which is good if you have gotten into the black-and-white, right-and-wrong thinking that sometimes comes with disordered eating. Art rises above all that.

Religion or Belief in a Higher Power

Many people find comfort, strength, and inspiration when they connect with God, or what they might call a "Higher Power," through religious practices and faith communities. Religious faith can provide a powerful framework for shaping values, actions, and choices. Some people prefer to be part of an organized religion, while others prefer to explore faith in a more individualistic, open manner. Either way, there is great potential for healing and growth by exploring a connection with a benevolent, loving, creative force for good that you can turn to when you're feeling weak and helpless. If you've had difficult religious experiences that involved judgment, condemnation, and shame, it can be hard to open yourself up to this type of spiritual expression. Remember: Faith by choice can be healing; faith by force never is.

Many different kinds of belief systems are available to explore, and you are entitled to search for one that suits you, if you like. How can you explore different religions? Visit faith communities and churches in your area. Read books about different religions. Talk with people you know who are part of a religion. Explore online. Take a class.

This chapter reviewed just a few ways that people have discovered to help them bring greater depth and meaning to their lives. What will bring a deeper meaning to *your* life is up to you to find out. The hard work of recovery is all about creating a life you truly want to be alive for. If incorporating some spiritual practices into your life helps, then why not give it a try? Of course, the choice of whether to explore spirituality is yours and yours alone. Give it some thought, and then proceed in a way that feels right to you.

Abiding Spirit

I swim through space.
I tumble over time.
I flow with grace.
I am divine.

To melt her sheet of icy pain,
I form a cloud of heated rain.
I soak up all her strength and ration,
then sublimate her rage to passion.

I find her sleeping inside her past,
reliving a dream which did not last.
I wake her gently to make her see
that only the present shall set her free.

I am the flame which won't go out,
the pain that can't be soothed,
yet deep within this heart of doubt
dwells the beauty of her truth.

I am her reflection, lo and behold,
I bathe in her shadow's sight.
I am her youth as she grows old,
her precious guiding light.

—Claire Bachofner

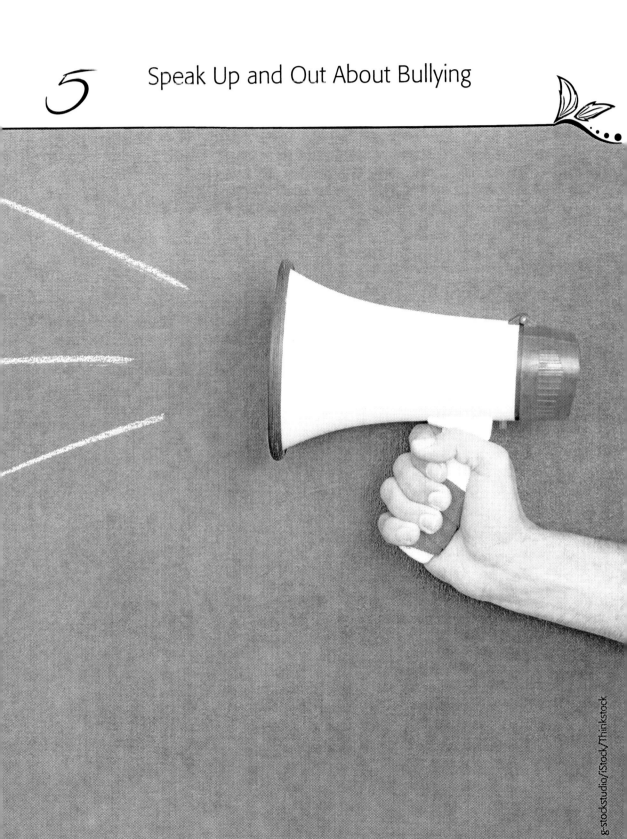

As you move toward health on your recovery journey from disordered eating, you may encounter people who are not living with as much honesty and intention as you are learning to do. Some of those people, possibly due to their own inner struggles, may freely share their opinions, judgments, and thoughts about you in ways that feel hurtful and damaging. They may even criticize, demean, belittle, and confront you with words and/or actions specifically chosen to cause you pain. In the past, such people may have even contributed to the circumstances that led you to seek the emotional distance and isolation an eating disorder provided, because you didn't know healthier options existed. Now that you are on the road to recovery, it might be helpful to learn positive ways to protect your emerging healthy self from this type of bullying behavior.

Yes, bullying. Unfortunately, bullying takes place not only on playgrounds and in school hallways, but in many other arenas as well. Many adults are the targets of bullies, and just as children can learn to stand up for themselves, so can you.

You are already standing up for yourself as you live moment by moment, bite by bite, in your recovery. As you move toward living a healthy, balanced life, you are standing up to one of the biggest bullies there is: an eating disorder—the bully within.

It might be helpful to compare the inside bully that is an eating disorder to an outside bully who tries to hurt and control people.

The inside bully:
- Doesn't let you eat food
- Makes you overeat food
- Tells you food is bad for your body
- Hurts your feelings
- Tells you you're not pretty
- Tells you you're fat, and that fat is ugly
- Takes away your beauty
- Makes fun of your true self
- Tells you no one will love the healthy you
- Takes away your friends
- *Would like to take away your life*

The outside bully:
- Cuts you down
- Tells you, or acts as if, you are never good enough
- Hurts your feelings
- Acts like a friend one day, and an enemy the next
- Shuts you out
- Seems to enjoy your emotional pain
- Belittles your true self

- Makes fun of your appearance
- Says bad things about you behind your back
- Is not a friend at all
- *Would like to make you think she can ruin your life*

See how similar these two bullies are? You can use many of the same skills to handle the difficult emotions that arise due to encounters with an inside or outside bully. Following are some specific things you can do when an outside bully makes an unwelcome comment about your appearance, food choices, or any other aspect of your life:

- Recognize that people who bully often feel insecure, anxious, worried, sad, unloved, guilty, or frustrated deep inside. They then channel those feelings toward others as an attempt to relieve themselves of their emotional pain. Their bullying behaviors are a reflection of their own internal chaos: it's about them, not you.
- Calmly, but as forcefully as possible, you can state the truth of your perception of their behavior: "I am (offended, hurt, saddened, shocked, stunned) by your words. Please do not make any more comments or do anything like that to me again." This is called setting healthy boundaries around yourself and how you deserve to be treated.
- You can choose to disengage by ending the conversation: "I am choosing to end this conversation right now because your behavior feels disrespectful. Perhaps we can try again another time." You can then walk away, hang up, or such.
- You can choose to speak bluntly: "What you just said/did felt rude and hurtful! Don't say or do that again!"
- You can compassionately observe what might be happening inside for the person: "You must be really hurting inside to say something that mean to me. I feel sorry for you." Whether you speak it or not, allowing yourself to acknowledge that the bully is hurting inside can help diffuse the emotional charge her words may have for you.
- You can counter with *your* truth: "That's not how I see it. I think …"
- You can ask for help if it continues or feels bigger than what you can handle right now. Turn to friends, colleagues, mentors, family members, or even professionals if you need help advocating for yourself and your right to be treated with respect.

Who Is an Advocate?

An advocate is someone who:
- Believes in you unconditionally
- *Can* speak up and out with knowledge, compassion, and understanding of bullying
- Provides support, guidance, and strength
- Will teach you positive coping skills to advocate for yourself
- Listens to all your thoughts, sharing your joys and your burdens

- Wishes you the best
- Accepts your authentic self
- Lends a shoulder when your strength weakens
- Delights in your successes and supports you in times of sorrow
- Is honest with you

Remember, just as there are bullies in the world and bullies in our heads, there are people in our lives who can advocate for us. We can also advocate for ourselves—with practice. You can become your own advocate by treating yourself with all the kindness, love, and respect outlined in this section.

Caring for Yourself After Standing Up to a Bully—Inside or Out

It can take a lot out of you to stand up for yourself. It's good to know that you can care for yourself after you do so, and you should plan to do so whenever you can. What types of things can you do? Whatever feels nurturing, calming, empowering, and loving. You could: journal, exercise gently, draw, paint, listen to music, dance, take a bath, breathe deeply, meditate, talk with a friend, or such. Whatever feels good to you!

Exercise:
- Think of a situation where someone bullied you. Describe it, including how you felt.
- What could you have done to stand up for yourself? How might things have turned out differently?
- Who are some advocates you could turn to for support?
- How could you nurture yourself after standing up to a bully?

By learning and practicing specific strategies for dealing with inner and outer bullies, you are doing two important things at once: protecting yourself from unnecessary pain and disempowering a bully. It will certainly help you in your recovery, and may even teach the bully a thing or two.

To Vanity

*We met
in a grocery store parking lot
where damp cardboard boxes burst with pumpkins
and the air was heavy with wet leaves.
You pointed, silently, to
a sobbing blonde
with a pretty face
and whispered,
"See? Even crying can be beautiful."
You had me then,
I'd seen your power
and I knew that you,
Vanity,
mattered most.
You moved in,
took up residence in my psyche—
flashed and flickered
through my thoughts
like a rickety old movie reel.*

*You taught me to pluck my eyebrows
on a static July evening.
I held my breath and watched
stinging tears well up
in my own eyes
and listened to the
distant sound of children playing.
I felt the light shift,
I longed.*

Behind me,
the sun melted
across the horizon.

In high school
we strutted down
hallways of chaos
and you pointed out that
anyone who mattered
was a friend of yours.

For you, dear Vanity,
I cashed in my health,
surrendered my sanity
to show you my dedication—
to thank you for what you'd
made of me:
a hollowed-out statue
a tiny, selfish figurine
just waiting to be shattered.

—Claire Bachofner

How to Help Yourself When a Loved One Struggles With Eating/Body Issues

The experience of loving someone who develops an eating disorder can be scary, frustrating, sad, and exhausting. You want to help, but you don't know how. You want to be an ally, but your loved one pushes you away. You worry, but it doesn't do any good. If this sounds familiar, then one thing you need to know is: you're not alone. Another thing you need to know is: you cannot provide the cure to your loved one's disordered eating. You can love, support, and encourage, but only the person with the eating disorder can decide whether or not to heal. What you *can* do is take care of yourself so that there won't be two people in the family suffering from ill health, and so you really *can* be an effective support person.

So how *do* you stay healthy and strong when someone you love and/or live with has an eating disorder? Following are some suggestions based on experience and current research.

Eat Well

Don't let your loved one's struggle with food influence your own eating habits. Keep a variety of foods in your house, and cook and eat well even if your loved one doesn't. Eat as healthfully as you can. If you don't know much about nutrition, learn. Read a book or visit a website, or talk to a nutritionist, dietician, or doctor. If you don't eat enough, or enough of a variety, or if you eat far too much, your body can't function properly. During this stressful time, you will need all the energy you can get. Sometimes, when people start to work on their troubled relationships with food and body image, it can trigger those who are close to them to evaluate their habits. Perhaps that has happened to you.

lola1960/iStock/Thinkstock

Don't let your loved one's struggle with
food influence your own eating habits.

If you discover you have some problematic thoughts and behaviors around eating and appearance, it might be helpful for you to consider delving deeper into your own underlying issues and decide whether you could benefit from making some changes. This is often the case, but not always, and it does not imply that you have somehow caused your loved one's eating disorder. It means you're human and, like many people in this culture, your eating habits could be better. The choice is yours whether to improve them.

Drink Lots of Water

This is another important fuel your body needs. Stay hydrated by drinking plenty of water to keep your body and brain running smoothly during this stressful time.

Exercise

Whether it's walking, running, bike riding, hiking, skiing, skating, yoga, weights, swimming, gardening, yard work, aerobics, dancing, tennis, racquetball, basketball, or other activities— just get moving! The benefits of exercise for good physical health are well-known, but the mental benefits are equally as impressive. If you don't exercise regularly, this is a great time to start. Regular, moderate exercise can provide a way to reduce stress, alleviate depression, regulate your appetite, help you sleep better, and give your mind a break. The key is to find what you enjoy doing, and do it. Don't worry about how good you are at it, or how you look, or what others might think. The important thing is to nurture your body with exercise. As is always advised, if you haven't exercised much in a long time, talk to your doctor for advice on how to safely start.

On the other hand, if you are a person whose exercise regimen is overly rigid, compulsive, and doesn't include appropriate rest and down time, you might want to consider consulting an exercise professional who can evaluate your routine. Just like anything else that is good for people in the right measure, too much exercise can wreak havoc on your body and mind, robbing you of peace and optimal health. Sometimes, people need to seek counseling to help them soften their destructive exercise habits.

Sleep

It's sometimes hard to sleep well when worried about someone you love. You can't function well without enough rest. Take it seriously if you're having problems, and ask for help from a healthcare professional. Organizations such as the National Sleep Foundation have websites with good tips for sleeping well.

Reach Out to Others

If there is a support group in your area, join it. If not, consider starting one. All you need is a place to meet, a regular time to do so, and people who want to share support, experiences, stories, and emotions. There are also eating disorder websites offering online support groups. You could reach out to family and friends. Choose people who won't judge you or be too quick to offer advice. Talk to people who care about you and who are good listeners. You don't need criticism right now; you need understanding and a safe place to express your feelings, whatever they may be. Many times, living with someone who has an eating disorder can be bruising to a person's sense of self. Out of their own pain, people with eating disorders may lash out in hurtful ways. By reaching out to others who are willing to listen, you can more easily resist the urge to battle verbally with your loved one, which will usually be pointless and frustrating. With a safe place to say anything you want to about the situation, you can be more in control when dealing with the conflicts that arise in the home. The resource section of this book includes some websites for online support groups.

Educate Yourself About Eating Disorders and Treatment Possibilities

Many resources for information are listed in the resource chapter of this book. You can also find information in your library, or at a local bookstore. Many colleges, high schools, and junior high schools have eating disorder literature and people in their buildings who can give you information. You could try looking in the Yellow Pages or online to see if there are any other eating disorder resources in your area. Nutritionists, dieticians, doctors, counselors, nurses, survivor mentors, and local health departments can be good sources of information, too.

There are many different ways for people to recover from an eating disorder. No one way is right for every person. In order to choose what's best for your loved one and/or family, you need to learn as much as you can. Don't let it overwhelm you; just take in as much as you can, and ask for help from professionals. An important note: when your loved one is ready to get help, it's crucial to find someone who has some experience with eating disorders, and with whom your loved one feels comfortable. It may take two or three tries before you find the right person or people. Sometimes, family therapy can play an important role in eating disorder treatment. Participate with honesty, respect, and humility if you are invited to do so. Open your heart and mind, and you might be surprised at how much you learn and grow from the experience. As for your loved one's individual therapy, don't pry, but be open if she wants to talk.

Avoid Weight, Food, and Body Talk With Your Loved One

Sometimes, people with eating disorders may tell you some of the unpleasant thoughts and feelings with which they are struggling. They may even try to pull you into the struggle, by asking how they look or your opinion of what they have eaten. Or, perhaps you have been in the habit of commenting on what people eat and how they look. As your loved one moves through the process of healing, she is learning to take responsibility for judgments about food, weight, and body image. It is seldom helpful—and often hurtful—to get into discussions about food and/or appearance with anyone, let alone someone who has an eating disorder. Instead, learn to see such talk from them as a sign of stress or distress, and perhaps offer compassion and caring instead of talking about their negative feelings about themselves.

Also, practice restraint, and resolve to make no comments about what people eat, when they eat, how they look, their weight, and the like, or about your own food and body image issues, which can trigger a negative reaction in your loved one. Of course, this doesn't mean you can't invite them to eat with you or tell them a certain color looks nice on them, but shy away from anything that could be taken as a criticism or judgment. The truth is that people with eating disorders carry inside them a constant critic whom they are trying to learn to silence. Let them hear words of love, encouragement, support, and faith from you, even though they might not seem to appreciate it. Someday, they will.

Note: If your loved one is very young and you are following a model of treatment that is family-directed, such as the Maudsley Approach, you will be expected to take a more direct approach with your loved one. In that case, follow the instructions of your child's therapist about what to say and how to say it. The preceding instructions are for those whose loved one is in more individualized treatment.

If It All Gets to Be Too Much, Seek Professional Help

See a therapist, counselor, social worker, minister, survivor mentor, or other helping professional. If you don't know of a good one, ask around. Perhaps your doctor could recommend someone. Check the phone book, or search online. If you don't click with the first person you meet, try someone else. A professional support person can provide great help when you've lost objectivity, or hope, or you're just plain out of steam. They can also help you process any difficult emotions that may be arising. Living with someone who has an eating disorder can be extremely stressful, frustrating, and scary. Remember: you're no help to your loved one if you're exhausted and stressed out. Deal with any issues that are troubling you so that you can be there for the ones you love, and for yourself.

Take Time to Nurture Your Inner Spirit

Most people lead busy lives, but it's important to carve out time to nurture the inner you: your spirit. How do you do that? There are many ways; find what works for you. If you're already involved in something that bolsters your spirit, stay involved with it. If you're not, explore some creative or spiritual outlets such as: writing, reading, meditation/prayer, artwork, time in nature, music, dancing, sports, or the like. It needs to be an activity that, while you're engaged in it, you sort of lose yourself to it. Research shows that this kind of deep involvement in an activity can be very beneficial to your emotional health. In spiritual traditions, this type of intense focus is said to connect us to a higher power, to God. However you approach it, it makes sense. Strengthening the inner spirit is just as important as nurturing your outer body. In fact, it could be more important. While bodies break down over time, people's spirits can grow stronger and wiser.

Reflection and Meaning

Take time to think deeply about what is happening to you and your loved one as a result of an eating disorder entering your lives. Find a framework for expressing and working through your thoughts and emotions in order to seek the deeper meaning of it all for *you*. Get completely honest with yourself as you struggle to understand how you feel about what is happening, and to consider what you must do to help your loved one, and yourself, heal. To move beyond the pain of it all, and learn the lessons inherent in the suffering you are experiencing, requires contemplation. Many people believe that suffering can teach people in deep and meaningful ways. It is up to each person to discover the unique lesson in the suffering. You might write, meditate, pray, talk to someone, create artwork or poetry, tune in to music, or any number of things. It will be much easier to move beyond the experience if you can discover or create meaning from it.

Keep Up With Professional Obligations and Personal Interests

It's good to keep your energy flowing into things besides worrying about your loved one's eating disorder. It helps you remember who you are apart from being a support person, and can actually revive you from the inside out. Plus, whether or not your child or loved one chooses to recover, you will have to go on with your life. Make sure there's a life with which to go on.

Interact in Loving Ways With Other Loved Ones

It can become easy to focus only on the person with the eating disorder. Don't forget to keep your relationships with other family members and friends healthy and strong. Do things together that are fun and relaxing, and *don't feel guilty about it!* The love and support you nurture with important people in your life will help you—and them—face the stress an eating disorder brings. A person with an eating disorder needs loving, nurturing connections with many people. Keeping the support network healthy and strong is crucial to all.

Interact in Loving Ways With the Person Who Has an Eating Disorder

Having an eating disorder is just one facet of your loved one's personality. Don't let it become the *only* lens through which you view her. Try hard to recognize and nurture the positive things about your loved one. Spend time together doing things you both enjoy. Discuss other things. Maybe this is a good time to take up new interests together. Get creative about how to connect, and also be willing to give space if that is what your loved one asks for.

Sometimes, it can be hard to talk with someone in the grips of disordered eating. When my daughter was struggling, I [Carrie] would write her notes or give her a card expressing my love, my faith in her, share fond memories, and my respect for the hard work she was doing to recover. I never asked for or expected a response, and seldom got one, but when she recovered, she told me those written expressions of love had been lifelines to keep her going, and to keep us connected.

Another good idea is to ask your loved one how you can best support her recovery efforts. Some people want to talk and hug; others do not. Once you have been told how you can best help, respect those wishes.

If you have fears and darker emotions you wish to express to your loved one, share them with the help of her therapist so no one becomes overwhelmed in the process. As much as you want to, you can't "fix" the eating disorder or shock her out of it by the force of your anger or sorrow at the situation. Step back and remember that as hard as the eating disorder is on you, it's 10 times harder for the person who has it. A little compassion goes a long way—for both of you.

Advocate for Eating Disorder Awareness, Prevention, and Treatment

Check out the websites in the resource section of this book for ways to get involved in awareness and prevention activities on a community or national level. Whether you are comfortable sharing your own story or not, there are many ways to become involved in helping people understand the truth about eating disorders. One place to start is National Eating Disorders Awareness Week held in February of each year. The National Eating Disorders Association website can give you more information. Your own healing might be helped by actively working for change in the larger culture.

Let Go

Let go of past notions of who your loved one is or was, along with your vision of who you thought she would become. People need freedom to understand how to find their way out of their eating disorders, and to envision a future in which they can live without it. If you feel sad, angry, frustrated, or disillusioned to realize your loved one is going to be a totally different person than you thought she was going to be, then go somewhere safe and experience those emotions.

Grieve the loss of a future you had thought would be. You must do that in order to truly let go and give your loved one the freedom and respect to be whoever she needs to be to stay healthy and strong. Let go of your old dreams for your loved one, and support her dreams. Let go of trying to "fix" a person with an eating disorder. It's not within your power. Let go of wishing it wasn't happening to your family. It is happening, and you have to accept that in order to deal with it. Let go, too, of guilt, shame, and blame; embrace forgiveness, honesty, and compassion. Let go of thinking you have all the answers; ask for help when you don't. Let go of controlling how it all will work out. Eventually, you'll need to let go of the pain your loved one's eating disorder has brought into your life. If you can't do it yourself, seek help.

Will your loved one fully recover from her eating disorder? No one can tell you that, but research shows that, with professional help, love, and support, there is a very good chance that she will. Stay hopeful, take it one day at a time, and take care of yourself. You *can* do this.

Daily

I remember the morning
I said goodbye to baths.

Good morning, 1988.

The hospital-blue shag
of the tattered bathmat
peeks between my tiny toes
as I wait anxiously,
paused and alert,
at the edge of a new era.

I'm exposed and shivering,
eyes on you, when you
crank the faucet and pull the lever.
The soft gushing stream
vanishes then reappears
hissing and spitting from above.
You step right in like
this is no big deal—
I have my doubts.

Inside, your voice echoes and curls around me
like steam, this all seems familiar, a warm rain.
I feel older, now.

Safe in the low light of your shadow,
I gaze up at a body I know better than my own
and watch drops of water meet your skin.
They shimmy down and branch off—
raindrops on a window pane.

Squeezing the shampoo into my open palm
your eyes meet mine,
"The size of a quarter" you say,
and from your tone, I know this is crucial.
"Now gather your hair into a little nest."
And I do, I copy every lathery movement,
reflecting your actions back at you,
our identities begin to merge.

We couldn't have known, then,
on a bright Saturday morning,
thousands of showers ago,
that, every day, I would look back
past all the broken years,
all your mistakes and mine,
to find (embedded in daily ritual)
this coin of memory
a shining image:
my mother's thick black hair,
a bundle of suds,
and our bond would burn in me.

—Claire Bachofner

Appendix: An Overview of Mentoring

Mentoring can provide:

- Commitment, knowledge, and life experience of an eating disorder survivor
- Support, strength, and guidance to help you balance your relationship with life and food
- Education of positive behavioral coping skills designed to fight disordered eating thoughts and behaviors
- Constructive feedback and observations to motivate hope, health, and healing for your disordered eating
- Someone who cares deeply to support and inspire your recovery goals

When an eating disorder survivor shares her real story, it brings true understanding to another person's healing journey. When I [Barbi] begin my healing work as a mentor, I share my personal story in and out of anorexia and bulimia. Unless you have experienced the thoughts and behaviors that consume a soul's life during an eating disorder illness, you cannot possibly know how awful it feels. A survivor-mentor truly can relate to a person with an eating disorder and share in the deepest revelations of honest "been there, done that" knowledge. The mentor knows a way out! She can bring bite after bite of healing support.

A mentor can share positive, life-saving cognitive and behavioral skills. If you practice them consistently, you learn not to give up and are empowered to heal. You will feel the great triumph of positively rerouting your relationship with food, life, stress, body image, self-esteem, and absolutely enjoying being yourself for maybe the first time.

Often, at the beginning, eating disorder sufferers don't tell the truth when asked questions such as how often they have thrown up in a week. Sneak, hide, and lie are still the easy way out, and needed to maintain "perfection." Unrealistic, irrational self-expectations, parent expectations, home life dysfunction, and life trauma call for more positive coping skills that a good mentor will share to help tackle the eating disorder lies and sabotage head on.

Do you have an eating disorder mentor? Please find one. There are lots of mentors out there, sometimes a little hidden, but definitely discoverable. This relationship is one of the most profound treasures you can give yourself as you heal. A mentor may understand better than anyone what is going on inside your head and body. She will be able to walk beside you and enhance your daily healing by sharing her experience. A mentor wants to give to others the second chance that she was given. She wants to make a difference in a suffering soul's recovery. Reach out and relish what the two of you share: a unique healing relationship.

A Note for Mentors

Mentors have the important responsibility to step up and advocate for a client's healing when they clearly recognize it and are strong now in their own recovered states to fight. Offer to walk beside the person and share your strength, including talking honestly about the fact that you recognize sneak, hide, and lie behaviors. Encourage a new direction or help draft a letter talking openly about parent expectations. Communicate about your work with the client's counselor (with your client's permission, of course). For the client's healing, you need to be honest and unafraid to bring things up because it is important that the eating disorder patterns are confronted. It is important for mentors to have the courage to tackle the eating disorder to do the best work possible alongside a client on her healing journey.

Resources

Eating Disorders Education, Awareness, Prevention, and Treatment Information

National Eating Disorders Association: http://www.nationaleatingdisorders.org

Anorexia Nervosa and Associated Disorders: http://www.anad.org

Binge Eating Disorder Association: http://bedaonline.com

Eating Disorder Hope: http://www.eatingdisorderhope.com

Mirror, Mirror: http://www.mirror-mirror.org

Eating Disorders Resource Catalog: http://www.edcatalogue.com

   This website and catalog offers numerous books, articles, and treatment center information about all aspects of eating disorder awareness, prevention, and treatment.

The Alliance for Eating Disorders Awareness: http://www.allianceforeatingdisorders.com/portal/#.Uo0_46VgzR0

Online Eating Disorder Screening

These sites offer a confidential online screening to help you decide whether to seek professional help for an eating disorder diagnosis.

National Eating Disorders Association: https://www.mentalhealthscreening.org/screening/NEDA

Eat-26 Self-Test: http://www.eat-26.com/

PsychCentral Eating Attitudes Test: http://psychcentral.com/quizzes/eat.htm

Advocacy and Cultural Change Information

Eating Disorders Coalition: http://www.eatingdisorderscoalition.org/index.htm

National Eating Disorders Association: http://www.nationaleatingdisorders.org/get-involved

Online Support Groups and Chats

National Eating Disorder Association: http://www.nationaleatingdisorders.org/find-treatment/support-groups-research-studies

National Eating Disorder Association (Family and Friends Network): http://www.nationaleatingdisorders.org/parent-family-friends-network

Mirasol Eating Disorder Support Group: http://www.mirasol.net/support

Sensible Nutritional and Mindful Eating Information

Recovery Today: http://www.eatingdisordersrecoverytoday.com/cat/nutrition_hotline.html
The Center for Mindful Eating: http://www.thecenterformindfuleating.org
RD 4 ED: Nutrition Help for Eating Disorder Recovery: http://rd4ed.blogspot.com

Recovery Blogs and Sites

Jenni Schaefer: http://www.jennischaefer.com
ED Bites: http://edbites.com
Karen R. Koenig: http://www.karenrkoenig.com/blog
The Body Positive: http://thebodypositive.org
We Are The Real Deal: http://wearetherealdeal.com

A Note About Sources That Promote Disordered Eating

There are people so enmeshed in their eating disorders that they try to pull others in with them by promoting anorexia and/or bulimia on the Internet or in other media. There may be many reasons for this: loneliness, seeking support for their illness, desire for attention (which could actually be a cry for help). Visiting websites or blogs, reading magazines, and watching videos that promote anorexia and/or bulimia will only encourage the self-destruction of the people who create them—and will feed those dark urges in yourself.

There are many positive recovery-oriented websites and resources that you can turn to for real support. Check out the ones listed in this section, and stay away from those that might hurt you.

Mentoring Resources

MentorConnect (a national online mentoring organization): http://www.mentorconnect-ed.org/
Body Balance (a Montana-based mentoring program that co-author Barbi Webber is a part of): https://www.kalispellregional.org/summit/nutrition/body-balance

Philosophy Websites

Internet Encyclopedia of Philosophy: http://www.iep.utm.edu/
History of Philosophy: http://www.friesian.com/history.htm
Wisdom's Haven: "Dare to be Wise!": http://www.wisdomshaven.blogspot.com/

Art Websites

Khan Academy: http://www.khanacademy.org/humanities/art-history-basics.html

Free Online Art Classes: http://www.free-online-art-classes.com/learn-about-the-artist-within-you-introductions.html

Artists' Journals: How to Create and Keep an Art Journal: http://www.artistsjournals.com/instruction.htm

The Fall

Strutting down a tangled path,
in steep and striking high heel shoes,
I'd fall with a grace I'd memorized.

I'd stay down as long as I could,
like a magician in a tank of water—
drenched and sinking.
Pain became my beloved teacher,
and struggle, my only peer.

When I walked through a crowd,
I'd stand tall
and display my endurance
like an enchanting tattoo
etched across my shoulder blades.

Each fall was the same
and amounted to nothing.
I'd lift myself up,
brush off the dust,
and set to work again
constructing a shiny new
set of circumstances,
a clean and fresh obstacle
to trip over
that would fill me
with more damage and loss.

When I performed the grand finale
it was too much to bear,
and as I hung in the sky,
suspended and exploding,
losing the last of what I loved,
my spirit began to tremble
and die down
and I knew it was all over.
This charade of fantastic failures
was finished.
And I surrendered:
every lesson I thought I'd learned,
each piece of knowledge I thought I'd gained,
all the strength I'd dreamt of having
and I just fell.

Delicious shock found me
when I landed in the arms of
a truth more solid
than any ground I'd walked on.

And there I remained,
still and sobbing
and changed forever.

As I listened carefully,
I understood:
I'd never have to fall again.

—Claire Bachofner

About the Authors

Barbi Webber, Mentor

Barbi Webber, BSW, CHWC, received her bachelor's degree in social work from The University of Montana and is a member of the National Association of Social Workers. Barbi is a survivor of anorexia and bulimia. For more than 30 years, she has mentored individuals suffering from disordered eating. She brings motivation inspired by the positive behavioral skills she created to find her own way out of an eating disorder. Barbi is a motivational speaker on behalf of body image and eating disorder education, awareness, and prevention from a survivor's point of view.

In her spare time, Barbi cherishes playtime with her family and friends, walking, camping, and prayer meditation.

Carrie Thiel, Licensed Clinical Professional Counselor

Carrie Thiel, MA, LCPC, has been a mental health counselor since earning her MA from The University of Montana in 2010. She opened a private practice in Kalispell, Montana, that same year, and continues to operate it currently. Before becoming a counselor, Carrie taught high school English for 13 years. In addition to earning a BA in English from The University of Montana in 1995, Carrie also obtained an MAT degree from Grand Canyon University in 2002.

Carrie's professional interest in eating disorders grew as a result of supporting her daughter through recovery from anorexia more than 10 years ago. As a teacher, she helped develop a program for at-risk youth and cowrote curriculum used in the program. Carrie has published essays, book reviews, and poetry in various magazines and journals.

In her spare time, Carrie enjoys reading, writing, watching documentaries, walking, dancing, yoga, and spending time with family and friends.